CURSE AND CURE

by Sabrina Scott

CURSE AND CURE

MAGIC FOR REAL LIFE

by Sabrina Scott

This book was conceptualized, written, illustrated, and designed by Sabrina Scott.
All contents in this book are copyright Sabrina Scott, 2022.
Photographs of Sabrina are by Ana Shahnovich, 2022.
Self-published.

For any and all inquiries please email sabrinadraws@gmail.com
or hello@sabrinamscott.com

Disclaimer: I deeply believe in the principles and teachings in each course, workshop, and book or other writing or teaching I offer. I teach sincerely and from my own experience. Success stories I share from students are from real live people who have worked with me through any of my programs and got fantastic results. I share my own life experience honestly, and the material presented in this book is my opinion due to my life experience. According to my lawyer, I need to make sure I always say this to you: I don't guarantee or warrant results or increased income. The testimonials I share may not be typical for all students. Legally I have to tell you that this book does not contain medical, mental health, legal, financial, or other advice, and that this is a work meant for entertainment. Please consult medical, mental health, financial, and legal professionals should you require their services. I am not accredited or certified in any of those fields.

A WITCH WHO CAN'T CURSE CAN'T CURE   A WITCH WHO CAN'T CURSE CAN'T CURE   A WITCH WHO CAN'T CURSE CAN'T CURE   A WITCH WHO CAN'T CURSE CAN'T CURE

Table of Contents

INTRODUCTION: HOW TO BE A WITCH
~~INTRODUC~~ INTRODUCTION: ~~HO~~ HOW TO BE A WITCH
- TAKE FLIGHT
- ORIGIN STORY
- WITCH BODIES
- BOUNDARY WORK
- THE EMBODIED AND EXPERIMENTAL SELF

CHAPTER ONE: PREPARING FOR MAGIC
- WHAT IS MAGIC?
- WHO IS A WITCH?
- CAN I BE A WITCH?
- HOW I SPEAK ABOUT MAGIC
- A WORD ON WORDS
- WITCHCRAFT AND MAGIC TODAY
- ARCHETYPES, HISTORY, AND STIGMA
- WITCHCRAFT IS NOT WELLNESS
- ACCOUNTABILITY AND RESPONSIBILITY
- SAFETY
- FREEDOM
- RISK
- CONSENT
- ETHICS

CHAPTER TWO: ENERGY WORK

WHAT IS ENERGY?
ENERGETIC CONSENT
WAYS OF SENSING
CLAIRVOYANCE
CLAIRSENTIENCE
CLAIRALIENCE
CLAIRAUDIENCE
CLAIRCOGNIZANCE
CLAIRGUSTANCE
TOO OPEN, TOO CLOSED
ENERGETIC NOTICING
INTUITION OR NEUROSIS?
ENERGY WALKS
INSTIGATING ENERGETIC SHIFTS
SHIFTING BY VISUALIZING
SHIFTING BY SWEEPING
SHIFTING WITH PLANTS
SHIFTING WITH STONES
SHIFTING WITH SOUND
SHIFTING WITH MOVEMENT
SHIFTING WITH LIGHT
SHIFTING WITH SMOKE
THE MAGIC OF SELF-CARE
GROUNDING ENERGY
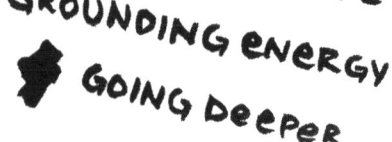 GOING DEEPER

GROUNDING WITH AIR
GROUNDING WITH FIRE
GROUNDING WITH WATER
GROUNDING WITH EARTH
GROUNDING WITH SPIRIT

SHEILDING ENERGY
CLEANSING
CLE
CLEANSING
CLEANSING

Chapter Three: Magic and You

Magic as Collaboration
Connecting with Yourself
Who Are You?
Where Are You Now?
Where Have You Been?
Situated and Oriented
Where Do You Want to Go?
Connecting with Culture
Understanding Who You Are
Appreciation and Appropriation
The Question of Eclecticism
Blood Family and Adopted Family
Walking Softly: Respect
Walking Deeply: Rigour

CHAPTER FOUR: CULTIVATING A SPIRITUAL TEAM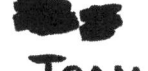

- CONNECTING WITH SPIRITUAL BEINGS
- TYPES OF SPIRIT CONNECTIONS
- ANCESTOR PRACTICE
- BLOOD FAMILY ANCESTORS
- CHOSEN FAMILY ANCESTORS
- COMMUNITY ANCESTORS
- THE HOLY AND HELPFUL DEAD
- MALIGNANT SPIRITS
- SAINTS, ANGELS, AND MORE
- DIVINITIES
- ASSEMBLING YOUR TEAM

Chapter Five: Objects, Place, and Magic
Altar Practice   Magic
What is an altar?
Altar practice as ritual
Working altars
Altars of honouring
Altars of manifesting
What goes on an altar?
Offerings
Maintaining dialogue
Maintaining relationships

Connecting with nonhuman beings
Tool, being, or both? Using vs working with magical tools   Feeling what resonates
Collaboration and consent

Obligation
Magical tools: an invitation
To audit your home

Connecting with place
Coloniality and imperialism: settler witchcraft

Specificity of place
Being here
Place and magic
Can we rest-in-place? The ethics of retreat
(Be)coming home: more ethics of retreat

Chapter Six: Connecting with Humans

Finding and Building Communities

Seeking Connection
The Desperation to Connect
Healing and Harm in Spiritual Communities
The Difficulties of Spiritual Leadership
Responsibility, Ethics, and Harm
Benefits and Drawbacks of Group Practice
Do I Need a Coven?
Should I Start or Join a Coven?
Online Community

Chapter Seven: Ritual
What is Ritual?
Mundane Activities
Everyday Magic
High Magic, Low Magic
Low Magic
High Magic, Low Magic Magic
Intuition and Instinct
Stepping into Sponteneity
Chaos and Impulse
High Magic
Planning and Order
Organized Magic

Chapter Eight: Magical Timing

Lunar Cycles
- Waxing Moon
- Full Moon
- Waning Moon
- New Moon

Solar Cycles
- Sunrise
- High Noon
- Sunset
- Sundown

Daily Cycles
Weekly Cycles
Monthly Cycles
Astrological Cycles
Seasonal Cycles
Cycles of the Year

Chapter Nine: Magic in Action

- ~~Eat~~ Sample Solo Rituals
  - Morning Coffee as as Ritual
  - The Mundane Magic of Self-Soothing
  - Building a Self-Love Altar
  - Releasing Trauma with Little Rituals
- Community Witchcraft
- Sample Group Rituals
  - A Ritual for Group Healing
  - A Ritual for Reclaiming Public Space
- Creating Your Own Rituals

Introduction

How to be a Witch

Take Flight

What is a witch?

You'll get as many answers to this question as there are people aligning themselves with this word—which, these days, is a lot.

A witch is someone who works with magic in order to create change in accordance with their will —often uniting many wills, many bodies, many spiritual allies.

Witchcraft is based on relationships the witch has built with their collaborators—perhaps plants, animals, spirits, saints, bones, objects, skyscrapers, concrete, garbage.

It is practical, enacted; it is a process, a practice. It is a doing, it requires intention. Our tools may look different, the altars we bow at take different form, but it is all – and can be – magic.

A cornerstone of my spiritual philosophy is that magic is everywhere.

We don't just learn about magic from books about magic. If we do decide to make that choice, we're placing significant limitations on ourselves and our practice. Everything I read helps and feeds into and influences my magic. How can it not? I'm sure the same is true for you, too.

My most cataclysmic influences came from people outside of explicitly witchy spheres—academics, historians, philosophers, artists, poets—most of whom had nothing whatsoever to say about witchcraft.

The biggest 'book' I can recommend about witchcraft itself is life experience (corny, I know); the book of speaking to the spirits themselves, the book of putting your ear on the grassy earth or into the lake water and having a good listen. Reading books and talking to other people are great ways to improve our knowledge, but there are many aspects of magical practice that can only be learned by getting our hands and feet and faces covered in mud.

ORIGIN STORY

Writing this book has inspired me to think a lot about origins: about where I came from, about where my magic comes from.

I was always that kid who made collages of skyscrapers—and though I'm not necessarily a fan of the overflowing preponderance of vision boards these days, it seems I magicked myself into the world of big tall glass buildings.

For more than a decade of my time in Toronto, my apartment was bookmarked between skyscrapers and a big park, residential Victorian houses, rows of shops. Before that, I was a city kid who had never really been to a city; I was used to jumping over garter snakes and wading through the grassy plains of newly suburban Colorado, land in the midst of a rapid shift from wild prairie to housing development.

In order to escape my home life, I either went online or on long walks around the neighborhood. I remember finding a black widow spider in my basement. I remember my dad deciding to get rid of all the snakes in the massive bushes that skirted our cement front porch. He removed more than fifty. I remember leaping over snakes like hopscotch to get to my front door. I remember that the snakes never worried me all that much. I remember learning to be afraid of spiders; for so long, they never struck me as all that strange.

I remember my mother's cat, declawed, still caught birds and left them for us. She was fierce, unencumbered, wild. I remember my cat, who I bottle fed as a newborn after I found her outside in a box, never came home. For years I felt her ghost footsteps on my bed, coming to comfort me, perhaps not even aware yet that her physical body was gone. I heard she had been eaten by a coyote.

In my escapes and salvation, yes, there was the internet and there were books, but there was also the world of spirit. Alone, I learned to listen to the trees, the plants, the concrete slabs, the new buildings, boxy and made of brick, shingles, wood, cement, particle board. I learned to find community in the spirits of where I lived, grappling as they were with a rapidly shifting landscape, a suburb built more and more day by day. We dealt with change together.

My witchcraft may have been solidified in the city, but it was born in this weird liminal space, a place between places, like so many others in America, grassy plains hugging mountains, high elevation, new suburban homes, wild animals, and a kid trying to escape their circumstance, to imagine a way out of chaos into a future that felt possible, stable, full of life.

I grew up in Spiritualism. Before my age hit double digits, I was fortunate enough to have attended displays of physical mediumship such as table tipping and trance possession. I also attended message services and energy healing sessions where I learned to both receive and give, experiencing this process to be deeply transformative.

The world continued to look different, to shudder with breath instead of sit still.

It scared me and then became banal.

It deepened what I knew in my bones.

On my own, I befriended spirits of many different kinds. On my own, before I ever stepped into a Spiritualist church (or otherwise), I was what I would later learn is called an animist. I have always felt the energies of objects. I remember one day, in a rage my mother threw a magazine across the room – she had gotten it for my brother, and he didn't like it. I went to pick the magazine up and began to comfort it. She said, No, you feel bad for me, not the magazine. I thought about it and decided she was wrong.

I daydreamed about a better future somewhere safe. The land and its spirits kept me alive, held me in a container while I slowly lost my mind. I am thankful today and always for their protection, for their lessons, for their love. Magic is about relationship – and I see evidence of that in my life, in my still being here.

WITCH BODIES

Many seem to operate under the misunderstanding that witchcraft is an exclusively 'female' form of practice, either contemporaneously or historically. This is something I've always tried to address and dismiss, because—however much it may resonate with someone as an individual—it can also be deeply exclusionary to others, and give them the incorrect idea that they don't belong within witchcraft or magic, due to a lack of resonance with cisgender female identity.

When I first dipped my toes into witchcraft, I was an androgynous kid with short hair. I fluctuated between the poles of frilly ballerina and butch hockey player.

For me, gender has always been about flux, shift, and play (and, of course, has been a site of pain and injury, too). Many magical systems also acknowledge and engage with the complexity and breadth that is gender. That's actually one reason I love witchcraft so much: I find it to be so innately trans, so innately queer. One need not look further than the Temperance tarot card or Eliphas Levi's famous Baphomet to find ready-made examples.

My witchcraft comes from this queer and non-cis place, even though, after decades of feeling more androgynous and non-binary, I've bloomed into what feels like the brave reclamation of a deeply feminine womanhood: a space I was never really allowed to occupy growing up. There's nothing static about gender, about bodies; and the full breadth of embodied expression.

There is nothing innately cis female or even femme about witchcraft.

Whoever you are, in whatever body, with any relationship to your own gender and embodiment, I want you to know that witchcraft is for you. Whoever you are, this practice is for you! If you feel called to learn, if you wish to practice, please do.

The reason I care about this – the reason I begin this book with these words – is not just due to the inaccuracy of claims of gender-based exclusivity. There is a lot at stake here: as it continues to move into the mainstream, the story of what witchcraft is and has been should be correct, by which I mean: multifaceted, open, multiplicitous, plural, curious. It is not just for women and never has been; it is not just for cis people and never has been. Witchcraft is for everyone who wants it.

Witchcraft has also very recently been co-opted within the wellness industry by people who don't know very much about it. Witchcraft, though it can be deeply beneficial in our lives and can help us work through so many trials and tribulations, ultimately has nothing inherently to do with commonplace superficial stories about what it means to achieve the elusive concept of wellness or wholeness.

Wellness, health, and healing are so much more complicated than buying the right crystal or jumping around on a particular full moon at a particular hour when Mercury is in retrograde. It's often slower, meandering, with more twists, more ups and downs. I don't believe in quick fixes; they're often false, short-lived, or worse.

I do position myself as a teacher and a thinker within the wellness space. I love feeling good, I love healing, I love being still, being challenged, and taking care of myself. I love teaching others to do the same. But witchcraft in and of itself isn't really about wellness – even though I find spiritual, mental, and emotional wellness is often something that emerges once we begin to take our witchcraft practice more seriously. It's a happy byproduct, but it's not the point.

Boundary Work

Are we cutting the claws of this potent thing called witchcraft when we welcome all things within it?

Do we really need claws anyway?

I don't believe everyone is automatically a witch.

Similarly, not everyone is a mathematician, not everyone is a scientist.

Boundaries are often permeable, flexible. Boundaries can serve a purpose, can help us communicate, can delineate what we do and don't do, what we are and aren't about, what resonates and what doesn't. Boundaries aren't about being mean or exclusionary, holier-than-thou or 'my way or the highway.' If there is no conversation about the boundaries of something, it can be hard to pin down and deepen it into something both meaningful and rigorous, or even to help ourselves understand what exactly it is. Words cease to have meaning, and this is contradictory to the power of words, both in witchcraft and in general. After all, witchcraft can help us translate word into world as we work to manifest what we wish.

To be a witch, it is not enough to be a woman. It is not enough to be poor, to be marginalized, to be disabled. It is not enough to be seen as on outcast, as out there, as a freak, as a rebel, as weird. Witchcraft is not wearing black, liking the nighttime; it is not long flowing hair or pointy black nails, it is not your big ass pentagram necklace or dark eye makeup.

Witchcraft is not accidental. It is not an archetype or a symbol; it is lived in, it is felt, it is breath.

At the same time, I am but one voice of many, as I should be. Regard me, disregard me, it is up to you.

The embodied and experimental self

The concept of the experimental self is important in witchcraft and magic.

Let me explain: my intention here is to teach practitioners how to get rooted in the body first, as an anchor for learning and developing important skills that will form the basis of any solid magical practice.

Self is the starting point for all magical work; once we feel physical changes, we know our magic is working and we can enact it on a bigger scale.

We create ripples.

Waves.

We can ride them, flow, float, feel.

Our body, our self, our spirit, our mind – we are our most powerful magical instrument.

Witchcraft in everything I do; it permeates my body. I see everything, consume everything, read everything, hear everything, feel everything through the lens of magic and witchcraft and spirit work.

It's the filter through which all else flows, and always has been.

How to be a witch will differ wildly based on who you are, where you come from, and where you want to go – as it should.

In this book, my intention is to show you the world of magic through my eyes. Maybe you'll love what I have to say. Maybe you won't.

Either way, you have my deep gratitude for coming along for the ride.

I hope you will collect somee tools for your journey.

Preparing for Magic

Chapter One

Preparing for Magic

WHAT IS MAGIC?

Magic is art.
Magic is life.
Magic is poetry.
Magic is prayer.
Magic is communion.
Magic is solitude.
Magic is beauty.
Magic is destruction.
Magic is fluid.
Magic is electric.
Magic is flow.
Magic is expression.
Magic is connection.
Magic is still.
Magic is me.
Magic is you.
Magic is all.

WHO IS A WITCH?

Anyone can be a witch.

You can't tell a witch by how they dress or how they look. They might have big pentagram earrings and be cloaked in black, or not. They could be in a fire engine red Adidas tracksuit. They could be wearing Gucci sneakers. They could be a soccer mom. They could be a scientist wearing a lab coat. They can be a man or woman, gender queer, non binary, they can be an adult or a child.

A witch really can be anyone.

CAN I BE A WITCH?

Yes!

Yes, you can be a witch.

Anyone can be a witch.

Anyone can build a long-lasting and meaningful relationship with magic. In this book, I'll use 'witch' as a shorthand for myself and for anyone who practices magic with a similar mindset and structure to what I do, but truly, there are many ways to describe a relationship with magic: witch, occultist, magic worker, magical practitioner; maybe you prefer to work with a word from a different language, or a phrase used in your culture, which is different from my own. That's cool.

Yes, you can do magic.

Yes, you can cultivate a deep, meaningful, and sustainable spiritual practice. Whether you decide to call yourself a witch – whether for reasons of safety, empowerment, or resonance – is up to you.

My aim with this book is to give you some tools to connect with yourself, whatever spiritual beings catch your interest, and the world around you – and, maybe, other people too. Your witchcraft won't look like mine, and that's okay.

Your magic can look and feel just as unique as you are.

How I Speak About Magic

There are as many ways to speak about magic as there are to do it. You'll see me working with lots of different terminology and ways of framing and thinking in this book.

When I talk about my magical practice, I prefer to use a 'work with' orientation. I don't believe I 'use' deities or magical tools; in my world, we work together in collaboration, communion, community, and kinship.

I also conceive of magic as work.

Work: labour, effort, intention; gradual, not always convenient, not always easy, not always with immediate outcome.

I do magical workings, not spells.

I do spiritual work. I do ritual. I practice.

Is this all semantics? Maybe!

But words do matter. Words can help us illuminate and shape our practices both to ourselves and to each other. Words help us communicate, connect. You won't hear much about 'spellcraft' in this book; this isn't how I think.

Do you just love the terminology of 'spells,' spell work, spell craft – do you prefer talking about your 'craft,' rather than your work? Do you feel you 'use' your magical tools? Absolutely no problem. Go for it! Embrace those terms.

My point here is simply to offer a gentle reminder that words create worlds: how we speak can reveal our ways of doing and being; words embed how we relate to those around us, how we behave in the world, and how we perceive it.

Speak about magic however you wish. Create your own vocabulary.

But/and: notice that every word, every phrase, has the potential to be an incantation, a chant, a talisman, and shape the contours of your reality. Words, too, create; words, too, are ritual; words, too, have power.

Words, too, are magic

A Word on Words

'Witch' is a contentious word, as is 'witchcraft' – and quite culturally specific! The names for varied spiritual practitioners and ritual specialists are many, and differ based on language, as well as when and where you are.

I'm not a big fan of mixing and matching terms, or of using terms out of context. In this book, I'll use the word 'witchcraft' as a heuristic to describe my own practice and my own perspective, which I share with you here: meanderings of magical forms and practices rooted in Great Britain, which have morphed drastically with their migration across English speaking countries such as Canada, the United States, Australia, New Zealand, and all over the United Kingdom and Ireland.

Even if you couldn't care less about the specificities of Gerald Gardner's birthing of Wicca, it's hard if not impossible to divorce its influence from magic in the English speaking world. English is my only language, and my inspirations, readings, and experiences are shaped by conversations happening in this context.

This book strives to be practical and non-denominational. That is, my desire is for it to be useful to you no matter what your culture, your belief system, and your experience (or lack thereof) with magic. What I have to say is, of course, rooted in my own cultural context and my own life experiences. If I make suggestions that don't resonate with you, feel free to throw them out, and adapt what does. Magic is nothing if not creative, experimental, and exploratory; I hope what I share here connects you to freely embody this part of yourself, no matter how hidden it may be.

I'll use the words 'magic' and 'witchcraft' largely interchangeably in this book, because this usage is true to me, but strictly speaking, these words are not synonyms.

Witchcraft, often used to refer to folk practice and land-based magical doings, is but one form of magic. People who practice ceremonial magic and highly ritualized forms of magic very rarely will solely refer to themselves as witches – they may use other words, such as occultist or ceremonial magician. Though I will briefly address ceremonial ways of doing, these are not the focus of this book. It may be useful to think of 'magic' as a big tree, with witchcraft as one limb, which blooms into many branches, which hold leaves and flowers of various shapes and colours, all referred to by different names.

WITCHCRAFT AND MAGIC TODAY

Witchcraft – what it is, what it looks like, who does it – has changed a lot over the years, and with the rise of a globalized social media culture, the practice continues to evolve. Witchcraft used to be far more underground, and a lot less public, than it is in our present moment. It's even become a little trendy in some circles to self-describe as 'witchy,' regardless of whether or not people using that word actually understand what it means in a literal, practical sense (rather than the symbolic). The witch has become a symbol of edginess, counterculture, feminism, and the hope of the oppressed, though it is not actually inherently about any of that.

With so much fog online, it can be hard to find authentic practitioners who take what they do seriously, and who practice what they preach... and actually get results! When it's more common to encounter fashion witches, or people in it purely for politics, aesthetics, or cool/weird/eccentric points. One benefit of social media, though, is it's a lot easier to find the folks you will resonate and connect with – whether their practice is similar to yours, or a completely different tradition.

Still, be wary of what you see on social media – there's a ton of people masquerading as experts with quick reels and infographics. When possible, read books, do research, and keep it moving. Touch in with your intuition, and be open to reading scholarly work about witchcraft, written by anthropologists and historians, and other academics in order to keep your feet firmly rooted in the earth. Be open minded, but not so open minded that your brain falls out through your ears.

ARCHETYPES, HISTORY, AND STIGMA

People have revered and loved practitioners of the magical arts as often as they have been scared of them. Witches and others like us have struck fear into the hearts of folks unfamiliar with our workings, as well as those who know enough to know they may have reason to be afraid.

Historically and globally, witches have been massacred excessively, with numbers ranging in the tens of thousands to the hundreds of thousands, depending on whose numbers you trust. This still does occur in some regions of the world today; it's not always safe to be a witch.

Similarly, many have felt that it's not safe to be known to witches – it is, after all, a belief in the efficacy of magic and witchcraft that makes witches an object of fear. There are generally two categories of people unafraid of magic: those who know how to do magic with great skill (and thus know how to protect, deflect, and fight back against whatever's thrown their way), and those who don't believe in it.

I'm not too bothered that witchcraft isn't illegal where I live. I'd rather be protected and safe from the law due to my culture's general disbelief in magic, than at risk of being put to death for practicing witchcraft.

In this case, I'd rather not be taken seriously in what I do: it is, sometimes, a much safer place to be.

Witchcraft has been romanticized, thought of as both dangerous and sexy (and maybe even a little bit evil), as well as ignorant, childish, and silly. It's sometimes hard to navigate these differing takes as a contemporary practitioner in the West; documentaries about people who do magic tend alternately to minimize, lampoon, misrepresent, sexualize, and other the practice.

The word 'witch' has been used to delineate the boundary between correct and incorrect religion, between truth and delusion, between the rational and the insane.

In the contemporary west, witchcraft has also been associated with women engaged in feminist activism; personally, this archetype does nothing for me. Am I a feminist? Totally, but/and I strongly believe that reducing witchcraft to an activity for women seeking to feel more empowered is an immense disservice to everyone. Magic has been practiced by all people, all genders, and also people of all social classes. Magic isn't only a tool of the oppressed – it never has been only this.

Can magic help people feel connected to their power? Absolutely. But magic isn't and has never been about overly identifying as a victim: it's quite the opposite.

If the archetype of 'woman equals witch' has helped you find your way to magic, that's awesome – I'm not trying to take that resonance away from you or anyone else.

That being said, these archetypes can essentialize all of magic, all of witchcraft, into something it decidedly is not: a fashion statement, a political statement, a public rallying cry.

The magic that I know goes much, much deeper, and can't always be summed up in a pithy infographic or superficial slogan.

There's nothing metaphorical about the magic I talk about in this book.

For me magic isn't a metaphor.

Neither is the word witch.

WITCHCRAFT IS NOT WELLNESS

Witchcraft is booming in wellness spaces. What used to be simply the new age movement— largely subsidized by divorced old white ladies looking to connect with their inner goddess—is now simply 'wellness,' so vague and inert as if to be completely meaningless, allied with the equally vague concept of health. And I say this as someone who has for the last few years described herself as a teacher within the spiritual wellness industry., so I really do see both sides to this, as well as the emotional allure and physical necessity of some movement towards wellness and health.

Before everyone freaks out, I'm not saying that care or wellness are irrelevant to magic! It's not.

Self-care is a crucial aspect of witchcraft.

It's a topic I've been writing and teaching on since 2012. However, I think it's important to remember that care doesn't always look like sweetness or kindness. For instance, justice processes for rapists and abusers are not often experienced by perpetrators as pleasant; however, this unpleasantness is necessary. These processes are ways of caring for survivors and communities, and ultimately for perpetrators as well.

Psychotherapy can often be jarring and unpleasant as we learn more about ourselves. Sometimes, what looks or feels violent or harsh can be a form of care and love, and can even be a part of stepping into responsibility and community. Care doesn't always look like flowers and rainbows – even self-care.

Witchcraft is not inherently about positivity. Witchcraft is not inherently about calmness, peace, or happiness. In fact, these goals rarely factor explicitly into my own workings. My witchcraft is much more often violent, chaotic, intense; intended to disrupt and instigate change where and when I least expected it, but where it needs to happen. The end goal may be personal growth (spiritual, financial, romantic, emotional), but we do often require dramatic and unpleasant shifts in order to get out of our own way, in order to step more firmly into the lessons we need to learn.

Spiritual bypassing—briefly summarized—is the tendency to spiritualify yourself out of any challenging or difficult emotion, which are often coded as negative.

Instead of working through emotions, they are jumped over, like a hurdle in an obstacle course. This involves not looking at the past too closely, not examining our bad behaviors and the impact they may have on others. This means not accepting our own hurt and anger, the ways we've caused pain and absorbed pain. Why pursue 'happiness' in this avoidant way?

Witchcraft, in my opinion, should not be used as a tool of spiritual bypassing. When we work with magic to ask for happiness and good vibes only, we sidestep doing the real and difficult work of toil, growth, and transformation that is often necessary in order to feel greater and lasting contentment.

With witchcraft, we can face our traumas, our demons, the monsters that always already live inside us; the ways we have been hurt and the ways we hurt others.

We can face our nasty patterns, the holes we keep digging ourselves into, again and again.

We can see ourselves through others' eyes, through the eyes of our spirits.

We let go of what we think we want: the job, the relationship, the ring, the money, the sex, the love that takes one specific form.

We open to possibilities. We trust the universe to catch us.

We trust our ancestors to catch us.

We trust the spirits to catch us.

We trust our magic to catch us.

In order to be well, we must go through periods of being unwell.

We cannot magic away our trauma.

We cannot magic away our rape.

We cannot magic away our abusive parents or ex-partners.

We cannot magic away our tendencies to people-please and put ourselves last.

Yes, witchcraft can be a big part of these transformations. If we believe in our magic, it should be.

But witchcraft doesn't whisk away our pain, our memories, all by itself, like a quick fix pill.

It helps us feel—not go numb.

It helps us go deep. It helps us gain the courage to jump into the icy cold plunge pool, head first.

It helps us hold our breath long enough for that cold to change us, to create shift in us, in our bodies and our beings.

Magic is a welcoming of that pain, of that incubation, of that movement, of that transformation. Using magic to sugar-coat and oversimplify our lives with a wash of false positivity will solve no real problems. Witchcraft is doing a spell for happiness and then being fired from your job, having your partner break up with you, and losing all your friends—all within the span of a week. Magic with integrity and depth is done with the long game in mind.

Our spirits often know that it's the partner, the job, the friends, or ourselves that are in our way.

While these losses can at first be devastating, I think often we find ourselves the better off for them.

Witchcraft doesn't always feel good.

But, even in those icky moments, it can be good for us.

Witchcraft shouldn't be used to sidestep or ignore our own demons. Unfortunately, that is much of what we see in 'witchcraft as wellness' spaces. Instead, witchcraft can help us to take a big look and step through to meet our demons with joy and gratitude and acceptance, so we can actually process and work through these less than savory parts of ourselves.

Pushing our nasty bits deeper beneath the surface without excavating them just means they will be worse when they finally explode through the surface, both for ourselves and those around us.

Burying a knot isn't good enough.

We need to untangle it.

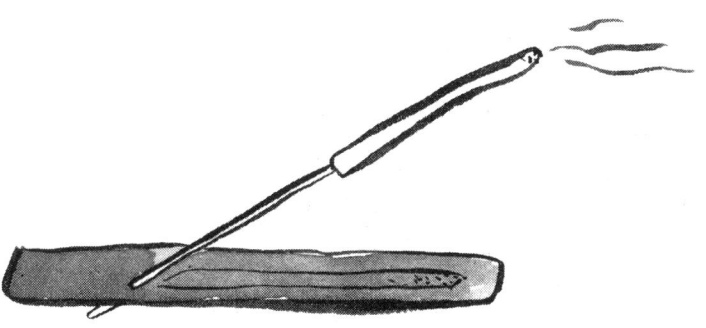

Accountability and Responsibility

We can't get out of accountability and responsibility in the spiritual area of our life. Yes, just because this is the spiritual realm, it doesn't mean it's a free for all without consequences or decorum. While stories of witch wars abound in community (which is a huge reason I took a big step back from participating in a lot of those spaces), you don't need to participate in that kind of ridiculousness. You get to decide what kind of witch you want to be, what kind of witches you want to consider your friends and community and maybe even coven members, and what kinds of magic you want to practice. We don't need to turn to magic for every little thing; we don't need to (and actually shouldn't) curse or hex everyone who slightly annoys us. If we do, that actually shows poor boundaries, poor emotional regulation, and an external locus of control - all things we'd be better suited to talk to a therapist about fixing.

What I'm trying to say is... magic is like everything else. If we whack someone in the face, they will probably whack us back, and may even be justified in doing so. But how do we react when someone whacks us? I've never cursed or hexed the people who have done me the most harm in this life, and though I'm not sure I ever will, it's not entirely off the table. It's important to be steady, measured, reflexive, and self-aware in our usage of the amazing magical and spiritual skills I'll be teaching you in this book. Protect yourself, stay safe, but be aware that there are often spiritual consequences - to you - if you get a little trigger happy with your magic.

Safety

Do you have paint in your house? Or – cleaning products, dish soap, hand sanitizer? If you're like me, you definitely do! These are everyday items that most of us don't think twice about having in our homes. We don't think of them as unwieldly or dangerous, because we all know – are likely taught, in childhood – that we don't put these items in our mouth; if we do, we might get sick. So, we all have these objectively very dangerous items in our homes, but most of us aren't that worried about it. We know not to drink paint, or nail polish remover, or dish soap, or whatever. We know how to work safely with these items.

I often hear of new practitioners worried that magic is dangerous and unsafe, that they might wildly injure themselves or explode their lives. And, it's true – they might. Magic can be a bit dangerous sometimes, if we don't know what we're doing. But the metaphor I like to teach with to elucidate the reality of the situation is this: most of us aren't taught the spiritual and magical equivalent of 'don't eat paint.'

Magic is a methodology, a tool, a way of life, a way of working and being. And if we know the magical safety do's and don't's, the likelihood of keeping ourselves safe as we traverse and experiment within the spiritual realms is higher.

Later on in this book, you'll learn about energy work. Energy skills are the foundation of magical practice. I'll teach you how to release nasty energy, how to protect yourself, how to summon good vibes to you. It'll take work, trial, and error to become confident and skillful in these techniques, but the best time to start learning is now!

FREEDOM

You are, of course, free to do whatever the hell you want. I'm not going to be sitting over your shoulder, judging you. However, just because you can do something doesn't necessarily mean you should. We're all free to spend our time to do what we want in this life. Our time is precious, both limited and expansive; it seems right to fill as many moments as possible with joy, growth, healing, and exploration.

That means – technically – you can do whatever kinda magic you want.

But should you?

Magic can give us a taste of freedom, of expansion. It can connect us with our souls, with ourselves, with our ancestors, with our resilience, with our past, with our present, with our futures. This is absolutely beautiful, and it can be life changing. I know it was for me.

At the same time, I find it can be helpful (and healthy) to think about what I do before I do it, particularly in terms of my magic and ritual. You may find these questions helpful to ask yourself:

Why do I feel called to do ritual at a certain time, for a specific purpose?

Is it a good time?

Does that ask even make sense – is it what I really want, and is it possible that I want something that isn't good for me?

What do my spirits think?

RISK

Nothing in this life is without risk. This is the case for magic and spirituality, too! When we learn to paint, we risk looking silly or unskilled (even if it's only to an audience of one, ourselves); of getting paint on our clothes, of spilling ink all over something. Sure, this is all pretty low stakes, but depending on where you're at, it can all be pretty scary!

Just as with learning to paint, in learning magic the risks we take – of trying something new, of being vulnerable, of maybe feeling a little bit silly or like a total faker – often pay off in spades.

When we think of risk, it's common to immediately think of putting ourselves willfully in the way of potential harm.

But risk is so much more than just risk of injury or pain: there's also risking success, risking transformation, risking getting good at something new, risking having a completely new life.

Risking happiness, risking expansion.

When we take a risk, it can go well, or it can go badly.

What if our risk pays off? What if, in getting vulnerable with ourselves and being uncomfortable, we learn something new?

What if, in taking a leap, our life starts to look different? Risk can result in ruin, but in magic I find this is rarely the case. The risk I hear most folks being scared of is, "What if, after I put in all this time and energy, I don't feel any different? What if I don't feel any energy or hear any spirits? What if my spells don't work right away?" They might not. You might not feel the vibes right away.

But with some persistence, dedication, and commitment to the process, I think you'll find that your efforts will pay off, and your risk of commitment will be rewarded.

CONSENT

When I engage in my magical work, I always ask for consent to collaborate with the beings I invite in. If I get a strong, "Sorry, not today," or even a "No, not ever, I don't wanna work with you" – I listen. I'll talk more about how to listen for that consent later on in this book.

A genre of spellwork that first comes to peoples' minds tends to be spells for love, or any other kind of magical working that involves persuading other people so you can get what you want. Sometimes consent may be implied, or outside the point of the working you're trying to do. If you're doing ritual work to keep yourself safe from someone nasty or abusive, obviously you won't be asking their consent; it would be like asking a home invader coming at you with a knife for consent before you whack him on the head. Sometimes, we're in a situation where it makes sense to defend ourselves and protect ourselves magically. Sometimes this defense may involve offense. Situations where this becomes necessary to think about and put into practice will be few and far between, but if you practice long enough, they will happen.

Have I done love spells without asking for explicit consent? Yes I have! But the circumstances were specific – I'd had conversations with the people I was dating at the time about what we were doing in our relationship, whether we were committed to one another, and whether or not we wanted to work on things – as well as detailed discussions on what those 'things' were. In these past workings, I was already in a committed relationship – and we both shared the same goals of getting closer. In those cases I've sometimes sweetened a relationship, or done workings so that we're both able to get over our own shit.

Does magic mean a relationship will last forever? Definitely not; in my own experience, working magic to help a relationship along can sometimes make the relationship come to a head sooner than it ordinarily would – and both parties can be faced immediately with whether or not they're actually well suited. In my case, this has always led to an expedited end of the relationship, which has suited me just fine – and when I've done relationship workings for myself when I'm in a relationship, I've learned the hard way to include a, 'or, if we need to break up, please force that to happen within x amount of time' clause. Whew. It's not for the faint hearted!

Some things to think about:

Would you ask for consent before defending yourself from someone dangerous? Likely not.

If you feel the urge to do a love spell on someone, would that relationship have any foundation that's even worthwhile? Likely not.

When I ask any beings to collaborate with me in magic – be they spirits, plants, animals, divinities, rocks, water, snacks, or whoever else – I listen for consent.

Later in this book I'll talk more about how to do this, within a framing of energy work and energetic listening. If this all sounds a little confusing right now, that's ok – we'll get to it!

What it all comes down to for me is: do the beings you wanna collab with also wanna collab with you? Consent isn't just for communication around sex between humans, it's relevant as a consideration around all interactions between beings.

Once this becomes a regular part of practice and awareness – if you want it to be – this is easy, simple, fluid.

Once spiritual relationships are solid and steady, negotiating consent around workings is easier.

ethics

Magical practitioners cultivate skills that allow us to shape ourselves, change our circumstances, and improve our lives.

Magic, then, is a form of power.

Studies have shown not that power corrupts; rather, power makes us more of who we already are. Kind, generous, ethical people with power just become more of all that good stuff; folks who have contempt for others and don't mind using and abusing whoever is in their way are likely to spread even more cruelty as they gain sway.

So, as a magical practitioner, there will come a point when you have to think about where you're at ethically – what you're comfortable with, what you're not, and why. Ethical frameworks run the gamut, and each has its own organizing principle(s); these are as varied as there are people on this planet.

You may want to spend some time considering your ethical stance on a variety of situations and types of magical workings – love spells, money rituals, protection, curses, hexes, and everything in between. Of course, many of us start out one place with our ethical compass, and when life hands us certain challenges and struggles, our stance can change.

Some spirits and deities are more than happy to work in the 'gray' area; others not so much.

You may think you feel comfortable dabbling in ethically dubious waters due to the desperation of your circumstances; when you sit down to ritual your heart may feel differently.

energy work
energy work
energy work

Chapter Two

WHAT IS ENERGY?

Energy is the basis of everything in magic. In order to ensure our witchcraft is successful, potent, and effective, a crucial first step is learning how to feel and notice and work with this fun little thing called 'energy.' That may sound intimidating—or maybe a little 'woo-woo'—but trust me, you've got this, and I'm willing to bet energy is something you've already noticed in your life, at least a little bit.

Have you ever thought about someone and then, moments later, ran into them? Or maybe you've walked into a room, be it a workspace, café, or classroom, and instantly felt sick and nauseous, or felt some kind of inexplicable weird vibe. Maybe you've met someone at a party and had a sinking feeling in your gut that you had to stay away from them. No particular reason, just a feeling. To the contrary, maybe you've instantly felt good around somewhere or someone.

All of these little noticings mean that you're picking up on energies swirling around yourself and others. We all have an energy signature: an essence or vibe that other people can pick up on. This energetic signature can be visually picked up with aura photography, a popular photographic technique that captures the energy field around a person. Energy can communicate a lot about where we've been, who we are, and how we're doing. Similarly, every object and place and animal and plant has an energy signature, or vibe, for us to pick up on and interact with. Energy can be big or small, thick or thin, friendly or otherwise, and everything in between.

Energy is all around us, and it helps to be aware of the vibes we bring to a space, as well as the vibes of what or who we are encountering or sharing space with! All of the beings that we welcome into collaboration with us have energy that they contribute to every working we do with them. If I do a ritual using candles and plant matter, each of those beings has an energy signature that they contribute to the overall energetic frequency of the working. Some may be more or less compatible with me, depending on how I'm feeling and what type of work I'd like to do. I may choose old candles I've had in my storage cabinet for a decade because they've been in such close proximity to me for ages, soaking up a lot of my energies, moods, and experiences, since by being around, they've gotten to know me over time, like old friends. Or I may choose brand new candles when doing work for a client, so it's energetically clear for both me and my spirit team that I'm not doing the work on or for myself.

Is our energy signature inherent? Can it be changed? Well, yes—to both. I have a certain energetic vibe that is mine, but it shifts gradually with what I'm going through. One purpose of energetic practices can be to get rid of any icky or unwanted energy that has latched onto us throughout the day or week or year, and to discard what isn't ours and what doesn't serve us.

This is also true for objects, such as a favorite clothing item we leant to an ex that they then returned to us. The same can be said for places, like our home after we expel a rude dinner guest or nasty family member. A big aspect of witchcraft and magic—if not the entirety of it—is learning how to first notice energy, and then to transform it with intention. Magic is about molding the energy of what is. Whether we want to summon up love, banish an ex-lover, manifest a new job, or unblock ourselves—all of this fundamentally comes down to instigating an energetic shift.

In order for us to shift energy, we need to feel it, and then manipulate it to do what we'd like it to do. This often involves a lifetime of practice, trial and error, failed attempts, big successes, and crazy explosions! Practice makes perfect (or nearly so), so don't get discouraged if you can't create these shifts immediately, or if the shift you asked for manifested in a way that wasn't exactly what you had in mind.

Noticing energy is its own skill set and language that needs to be built over time. As we learn a new language, for instance, our first language's accent may come across quite thick, and over time it may diminish as we gain fluency with the new-to-us language. Learning energy skills is similar. At first you may feel blocked or ineffective, not sure how to 'speak', but a lot of energy work is about programming, or creating clear instructions and directions for the energy we're working with.

ENERGETIC CONSENT

One facet of magical practice and process that is incredibly important to me is the concept of consent. Yes, consent applies to magic, too! In my book Witchbody, I discuss my worldview as it pertains to magic, so if you're interested in a full, in-depth discussion of my spiritual ontology, I recommend checking it out. In short, I see magical practice as collaborative. Magic as a process is not just the witch as 'lone acting body' (in this sense acting means doing things, creating things, instigating shift). Many magical texts and 101 books seem to take that attitude—that the witch can do whatever they want with whatever other beings they want. I find this approach to be extractive. If some books do include a section on consent, they often only mention the Wiccan 'threefold law' around ethics, which basically says that whatever energy you put out into the world, positive or negative, will be returned to you threefold.

One facet of magical practice and process that is incredibly important to me is the concept of consent. Yes, consent applies to magic, too! In my book Witchbody, I discuss my worldview as it pertains to magic, so if you're interested in a full, in-depth discussion of my spiritual ontology, I recommend checking it out. In short, I see magical practice as collaborative. Magic as a process is not just the witch as 'lone acting body' (in this sense acting means doing things, creating things, instigating shift). Many magical texts and 101 books seem to take that attitude—that the witch can do whatever they want with whatever other beings they want. I find this approach to be extractive. If some books do include a section on consent, they often only mention the Wiccan 'threefold law' around ethics, which basically says that whatever energy you put out into the world, positive or negative, will be returned to you threefold.

Whether or not we're thinking about engaging in magic for or with other human bodies, the question of consent is crucial. Where humans are concerned, we can ask directly. We can ask our partner if they mind if we do a ritual to help them ace their job interview, and we can ask our friend if they mind if we do a healing ritual for their stay in the hospital after surgery. This all seems rather innocuous, I realize, but it can be important to know that everyone involved wishes to participate.

Have you ever thought about asking your magical collaborators for consent to their collaboration with you? Or has it occurred to you that you may be forcing the participation of some herbs, gemstones, whatever it is, without considering whether they're the right collaborator for you, either in that particular rite, or ever? Whenever I am about to embark on a magical rite or ritual, I do my best to energetically 'feel out' the desire (or lack thereof) to participate in ritual with me that the non-human bodies in my life may have at that moment. I may crouch in front of my candle storage and slowly scan over all of the candles with an open hand, palm facing down towards the candles, and see how each of them feel to me. Some of them may be pushing me away energetically with a 'no, not now' type of vibe – and
others seem to jump out, as if saying, 'pick me, pick me!'

Sometimes I initially misjudge, and pick up the candle I think wishes to come out, and then feel a very strong visceral 'nope' until I put it back where it was and choose another. I use this same process when selecting herbs and gemstones; sometimes the names of collaborators will come to me and the energetic scanning process will not be necessary.

Why is consent important? There are two types of consent here: consent of the target, and consent of the participants.

If your magic is only as strong as your relationship with your weakest magical collaborator, it is good magical practice to try and ensure all of your relationships with the beings with whom you're collaborating are strong, stable, desired, and feel reciprocal to all involved. When doing magic, we want all participants to feel okay with their involvement.

I hate to use a sports analogy in a book about witchcraft, but there is a serious parallel here! If it helps, think of all of your collaborators as your magical 'team.' Peppermint leaves, charcoal block, copal resin, makeshift chalice from the thrift store, your lighter or box of matches—these are all your magical teammates. In order to work together and perform well, all teammates need to be on the same page. In sports, sometimes certain teammates sit out and don't participate, for a variety of reasons: maybe someone has an injury; or perhaps a family emergency; or perhaps even isn't called to play a particular game against a certain team because their skillset doesn't match up the best with the opponents. Whatever the issue is, sometimes it's not a good fit.

So, check in with your magical teammates, using any of the energetic techniques below, to see if they'd like to collaborate with you on a ritual or spell.

WAYS OF SENSING

Some of us are talented painters, with a knack for combining the perfect colors side by side. Some of us are perfumers, able to finesse the beauty of mixing two unconventional scents. Some of us may have an excellently developed taste palette, the skill to explain in excruciating detail the minute differences between a selection of wines or espressos. Each of us has some senses that are more developed, and some that are less so. We have our talents and our weaknesses. When we work with energy, we have the same things to consider—we have senses that are more developed, and some that are less developed, stuff that we just won't be able to pick up on no matter how hard we try. Often, when folks are blocked energetically it's because they're trying to connect with energy in a way that isn't the most natural to them.

Personally, my strengths in noticing energy are through feeling (a physical sensation in the body, often hot or cold tingles, generally in my hands or sometimes elsewhere), through knowing (a very clear conviction makes itself present in my brain, such as which incense or herb to use to banish a particular spirit), through hearing (words from spirits, whispered into my ears), and on occasion through sight (pictures in my mind's eye of spirits and what they are wearing, what they look like, or of certain situations or environs) and smell (sometimes I've smelled tobacco, perfume, or even the rot of dead bodies when no one else could). It is through these sensitivities and skills that I communicate with spirits, notice the energies around me, and also, crucially, notice how my magic either is or isn't working. It's a big part of how I choose my candles, my herbs, and how I choose to work with clients both in teaching them and doing workings for them.

If you've ever been to a public magical ritual with no soul and no heart, where people were reading from a "Holy Binder of Shadows," and where everything felt a bit more like bad theatre than a spiritual experience, you've been to a ritual that was likely conducted by people who were not skillful in their energy work. Learning to sense energy is like the ingredients in cooking you can't skip out on – and whether or not you've done the work can become quite obvious in your rituals and your relationship to magic!

Here are some common ways to sense and notice energy:

CLAIRVOYANCE

This style focuses on clear sight or clear seeing. If this energetic language comes easily to you, you may have had experiences where you either see spirits in your physical space, perhaps sitting in the chair on the other side of the room looking quite solid, or you might see figures or colors in your mind's eye. If spirits don't look as solid as incarnate humans do, but you still have an aptitude for visual pictures that pop up in your head, clear seeing may be a natural skill of yours. I recommend working with your mind's eye and developing your skills of visualization. Using visualization in your magical work will likely go quite well for you! I also recommend trying out visually-oriented divination practices, such as tarot or oracle cards. Clairvoyance often comes most easily for people who already have strong visual skills.

Clairsentience

This style references clear feeling or clear sensing, wherein physical bodily sensations give us energetic information. For example, I feel a hot or cold tingle in my hands when I am intentionally doing energy work – particularly when I am raising energy. If this feels natural to you, I recommend working with the energetic feelings you receive in your body as you encounter different spaces and people. What does a good vibe feel like to you? A bad vibe? What is the language or grammar of the sensations; do you notice any patterns or repetitions? I tend to get a cold clammy feeling in my gut and throat if a situation, person, or place will not serve me and my best good. Positive energy tends to feel warmer to me, like an expansive heart opening. If you'd like to develop your understanding of your own energetic impressions, try keeping a record. I also recommend checking out forms of body-based work, such as physical movement like yoga, running, walking, or Pilates, as a form of spiritual practice, or even something like reiki or energy healing.

CLAIRALIENCE

I love this one—clear smelling! I've had experience with less pleasant spirit smells, such as that of rotting flesh in a haunted room before I did an exorcism on it (seriously), but it's much more common to smell mundane, everyday scents like tobacco smoke, whisky, and even a favorite floral perfume of the deceased, perhaps with notes of rose or lavender. If this is a natural skill of yours that you'd like to develop, I recommend training your nose in the mundane world! Take a course on scent and perfume, or even try cooking with different spices so you're better able to discern the subtle distinctions between both sweet and savory smells, how each scent is distinct. The more developed your nose is in the mundane world, the better you'll be able to discern the intricacies of different smells when they come to you in spirit.

CLAIRAUDIENCE

Perhaps unsurprisingly, this refers to clear hearing. Do you sometimes notice spirit voices in the back of your head, or even a bit more loudly than that, where you'll hear something and turn around and there's nobody addressing you? Or perhaps a spirit song that no one else can hear, or even a little meow or bark coming from spirit? However loud or soft these sounds are, if you're able to hear things that other folks can't (and it's not attributable to schizophrenia or any other mental illness), chances are you're talented in hearing spirit. If you're not already musical or interested in voice, it might serve you well to further develop your ear and ability to listen and identify different sounds, tones, and accents so that you'll be able to better receive from the spirit world.

CLAIRCOGNIZANCE

Clear knowing is a skill I've explored with many of my clients, and it's something I also have myself. This style of energetic sensitivity is when we just 'know' something; this knowledge has no clear origin. I work with this quite a bit when I do tarot readings for folks: I will instantly know which parts of the card are relevant for who is sitting in front of me. I'd also describe claircognizance as having an incredibly strong intuition. If you'd like to develop this part of yourself, devote your time to studying intuition by reading books about it, and putting this into practice by actually listening to yours! Don't fight it off or dismiss it as silly or random—pay attention, say yes to it, and see what happens. I think you'll find that there's quite a few synchronicities that may surprise you. Be sure to record your insights to check later, to build your confidence and remind yourself you didn't just make it up!

CLAIRGUSTANCE

Perhaps the least common form of energetic sensing, this style is clear tasting, which refers to being able to taste stimulus from the spirit world. Do you already have a developed and advanced palette in the mundane world? If not, I'd strongly consider developing this part of yourself in the physical world by becoming more attuned to the subtleties of different flavors and tastes, both of food and drink, so your readings of what you receive through spirit will be more accurate and perhaps more fruitful when you interpret that information for yourself or others.

It is a good idea to take note of how spiritual information comes to you, and when it does. What form does it take? Do you constantly hear spirit speaking to you, or do you mainly see a video reel of images in your mind's eye (or right in front of you)?

If you can't relate to many or even any of the ways of spirit sensing discussed above, don't worry! You can still connect with it over time. I believe in you. Start by reflecting on your passions in life: do you love good food and wine, or are you happiest on the beach feeling the sand beneath your feet and listening to the waves? What senses do you particularly enjoy? What makes you happy? This process should be enjoyable—challenging, perhaps, but ultimately I invite you to have fun as you learn, and open yourself up to playing with your senses, both tactile and more ephemeral.

Too Open, Too Closed

Now that we know more about energy, we can look at the biggest problems folks often have when connecting with it. Clients who come to me for one-on-one spiritual consulting work often have one of two challenges: they're either far too energetically open, or they're far too closed, and can't connect with or feel anything.

The folks who are too open are often overwhelmed all of the time: they're exhausted, tired, have problems with headaches, dizziness, and nausea. Their brains and bodies are flooded with so many messages they don't know what to do, energy that creates a great deal of noise and commotion. They pick up on the energies of every place they go, every person sitting next to them at a coffee shop or standing next to them on public transit. Though folks who have a hard time connecting to spirit at all may initially feel a pang of envy, trust me—this problem is not all it's cracked up to be! One antidote for this issue is to create strong energetic boundaries and strengthen relationship with our spirit team. In this chapter, I'll show you some ways to do this.

The folks who are too closed have never heard a spirit, or have a really hard time feeling the hot or cold tingle of energy. They're often frustrated with their lack of feeling and sensation, and can feel broken, hopeless, and at a loss. They feel like they've tried everything and aren't sure why 'everyone else' is getting it so easily! Hot tip: Most folks aren't; it does take a lot of time and hard work! These people are often tempted to give up. But they aren't broken, they aren't incapable. It's just an issue that needs some untangling, and a whole lot of effort and commitment.

The problem at the heart of both of these issues is energetic and spiritual boundaries. The folks who are too open have almost no boundaries, or at least very little, weak, or easily breached boundaries. The folks who are too closed have boundaries that are way too high and strong, boundaries that are enforced past the point of usefulness. So, when I'm working with these individuals, an awareness of and proficiency with energetic boundaries is a big part of what I try to teach and facilitate. One purpose of boundaries is to help keep us protected and safe; however, sometimes we build a wall around ourselves that keeps even the good parts out.

Energetic Noticing

I conceive of energetic noticing as a practice of listening and feeling. Before we seek to shift energy, it's crucial for us to back track and see what the energy even is to begin with. What's the energy like in the room we're about to cleanse? What's our energetic state in our own body at the present moment —physically, mentally, emotionally, spiritually? Before we know what energetic shifts need to be instigated, it's crucial to connect with exactly where we are.

Do you feel revved up, or slowed down? Do you feel like you need to pull up some energy from the earth, or do you feel like you need to get rid of some? Does your living space feel peaceful and calm when you come home to it, or does it feel tense?

Take a moment to notice and observe your body and how it feels. Notice your mind, too. What's going on for you? Are you happy and high off a recent accomplishment, or is your being rife with the stress of a deteriorating relationship? Or, more broadly, where are you at in life right now? Are you on a trajectory you'd like to continue and push forward, or are you in a bit of a rut?

The places and bodies we inhabit are permeated by pulsating energy, all the time. Doing work for change and personal transformation—of both our communities and ourselves—is something that expends a lot of energy, and which sends a lot of energy out into the world. When we engage with energy without intent or awareness, we have the potential to create spaces which are triggering, unsafe, and hostile—spaces where it may be difficult or impossible to engage in the work we wish to do as witches and magical practitioners interested in diving more deeply into spiritual practice, and healing ourselves, our ancestries, our communities, and our environments.

This works on both a literal level and an energetic level. Is the room you are in comfortable? Is it sufficiently warm or cool? Do you feel safe? Is there adequate airflow? Sometimes, rooms just have bad vibes. I know that some classrooms, homes, and cafés I've been in make me feel nauseous and uneasy every time I'm there, if I'm not careful to protect myself. Whether or not that's the case with the space you're in, it's important to know how to work with and clear spaces with negative energy signatures. Sometimes we may not have another option than to work with those spaces – maybe you're a teen still living at home with your parents and things are a bit tense; maybe you're an adult living with roommates who have attitude problems, and you can't move quite yet. Maybe your boss has a chip on their shoulder. In all of these situations, energy work can help you protect yourself, and be responsive to the present moment.

After all, we can't discard our human bodies, even if we're in a lot of pain, or carrying a lot of trauma. Sometimes, we can't leave a situation quite yet.

We can work with what we have, and start exactly where we are.

No judgement, no shame.

Shift.

Process.

Manifest.

Change.

Create.

Connect.

INTUITION OR NEUROSIS?

One concern I hear often from my spiritual consulting clients and my students is that sometimes, they aren't always sure if what they're feeling is true intuition or their neuroses: anxieties, worries, fear, trauma response, hypervigilance, or even a fun mix of all of the above, and more.

Do you resonate with that? If so, I completely understand, as I've been there myself! It can be incredibly difficult to tune in to our bodies and the energies within and outside of us, and to do deeper work of discernment – especially if we're feeling invested in a particular outcome. I find when peeople start to teach themselves magic (or even tarot), often they're inspired to do so because they feel compelled to take action on something near and dear to their hearts.

I'll give a spicy and hopefully relatable example: Love!

Love magic is popular, as are tarot readings about love. Imagine you're brand new to tarot, and you pick up a deck of cards. You're excited, kinda anxious, and really want some answers to put your mind and body to rest. You shuffle them and think about your crush, who has been kind of a douchebag lately. But still, you're absolutely infatuated. You're not too sure if things have potential and they're just having a weird week – or whether you should call it quits. We've all been there!

You fan out the cards, face-down, and hover one of your hands over the top of the cards, maybe a few inches above them, not touching, just sensing the vibes. You try to connect with your cards and feel the energy of which cards are the correct ones to pull for your situation. Your hand tingles as you notice which cards are asking to be pulled and share their wisdom. You feel a bead of sweat roll down your forehead. You move your hand to the left a bit. Your stomach does a flip. But, wait – was that tingle a burst of intuition, or a shock of fear and paranoia? Sometimes, it can be hard to tell, especially if you're newer in your practice.

And, hey, even those of us with more experience can have some difficulty feeling out what's what when matters of the heart are involved. There's absolutely no shame in admitting that sometimes it can be challenging to discern which vibes are which.

This is especially true if you already have some difficulty touching in with your body and noticing how you're feeling, where you're holding challenging emotions.

Whether you live with something more serious and potentially destabilizing or stressful like depression, anxiety, or trauma, or are just having regular old worries or the occasional insecurity – we will all have moments of not being completely sure if we can trust ourselves, our intuition, and the vibes we're picking up on.

Magic, witchcraft, and spirituality are ways of being and working that I believe are best as parts of a larger ecology of support systems, which may include movement practice (hockey, yoga, pilates, dance, walking, etc), therapy (working with a psychologist, psychotherapist, or counsellor), and/or even a psychiatrist, naturopath, or mindset coach. I have worked with all of these at some point in my journey to keep myself balanced and grounded – it's definitely helped my magical practice to have these professionals work with me to address any underlying health and wellness concerns that can sometimes get in the way of really feeling into the energies around us. Cultivating mental and emotional health and wellness can only help our spiritual and magical practices. At the very least, it certainly won't hinder them.

That being said, it can be really helpful to develop an increased awareness of the language of our bodies. With an increased attention – which can emerge through practice and patience – you might notice that anxiety hits you in your stomach as a wave of nausea, and intuition bubbles up more as sweaty palms. Part of becoming an expert in this work is learning the difference.

Not every feeling we have communicates itself in the same way, and you'll likely notice over time how differently intuition can feel from anxiety (or whatever else ya got going on).

Do be patient with yourself – this noticing takes time! And it can be hard at first – which is why I tend to suggest that newer folks don't try to tap into intuition around more difficult topics where they have a hard time not being emotionally activated or stressed out as it is. Keep it simple to start.

Remember our love tarot reading example above? Instead of asking about love in that way, I'd recommend someone in that situation simply pull a card for whatever message it is they would most benefit from hearing that day. It's open-ended and not as emotionally charged – so, it's not stressful, and much easier to listen to our intuition in these cases, especially if we're new in developing our ear for magic and energy. Or, if we're feeling particularly stressed – in that instance I'd recommend reclaiming our connection to our agency and magical power through sifting through our tarot or oracle deck face up, and pulling out whatever cards speak to and depict how we want to feel, the energy we want to embody, to help us summon it into ourselves.

If you're having a hard time discerning between intuition and your own personal neurosis – first, take a break to refresh yourself! Reset. Come back to it later. Build your confidence in your own ability to listen to yourself by starting off with topics that aren't as emotionally charged for you, and practice your energetic noticing skills on topics and areas of life that are a bit more mundane and banal. In the next section, I outline an exercise I designed for my students, which I call going for an Energy Walk. This is a regular part of my own spiritual practice, and is how I maintain a connection to my own sense of self, place, and the beings all around me.

ENERGY WALKS

If you're having trouble discerning whether you're feeling actual intuition or something else, I have the perfect technique for you to practice your noticing skills! And, even more fun, it means you'll get to know where you live a little bit better, too. No purchase necessary. All you need is your body.

I always suggest my students go on what I affectionately call 'Energy Walks!' In my own personal practice, this is something I do – and I see it as an intentional form of walking meditation. No one is ever too experienced to return to this practice, myself included.

At the time of this writing, I've recently moved into a new-to-me neighbourhood in the city I live, Toronto. I'll go on walks for – depending on my mood, vibe, and energy level – anywhere between 4km to 12km, with no particular goal or route in mind.

Sometimes I know I'd like to go visit the water, or a little patch of forest or parkland. Sometimes, I'm in the mood to go walk past this really cute contemporary house on a far-away street, otherwise lined with Victorian homes. Other times, I want to only walk down streets I've never walked down before. I don't look at the map on my phone. I have no plan. I just walk. I don't think about it. I allow myself to walk for the simple joy of it - and as I walk, I attune myself to noticing the energetics of each street I walk down. When I meet a crossroads, I feel into the energy of each possible route. How do they each feel? There is no right or wrong here, just vibes – and that's a big part of why I love teaching this technique to my students.

With an exercise like this, 'right' or 'wrong' become moot – there is no correct answer, there's nothing heavy and stressful at stake – it's simply about learning about where we are, and the energies of the bodies around us (people, homes, plants, animals, soil, concrete, trash bins, and more) – which makes it a lot easier to release fear of making the wrong decision.

When we practice our energy work with something like this, going for a walk, and intuitively deciding upon our route, which street we walk down, we are free to step out of fear and worry about making the 'wrong' choice, and more into feeling the energies around us.

For me, this practice is about coming into a sense of place, of learning the energies and personality of my new neighbourhood – coming to know the energetic topography of the land I live.

As I've done this, I've noticed that different patches of forest feel different, different patches of water feel different - some feel more hollow, some more resonant, more like friends. Certain streets feel colder and standoffish, other streets welcome my footsteps like a long lost friend. Some patches of rock and water embrace me with open arms, happy to see me again. Other stretches of neighbourhood street encourage me to walk faster, to remove myself from their milieu.

This probably goes without saying, but please do have a working GPS/map on you, a functioning phone (even if you keep it on silent), and a few extra bucks – please don't walk anywhere where you are putting yourself at risk of harm. I know there are parts of my city where I feel safer than others, and I know we all occupy differently gendered and racialized bodies which are not always equally safe, and safety is never a guarantee, no matter where we are. I don't want this energy exercise to involve you putting yourself at risk, so please use your own wisdom and judgement, have your wits about you, and have tools with you to call a cab or other ride hailing service to teleport you home, if need be. If it helps you feel safer, do let a friend or family member know where you're going and when they can expect to hear from you.

My own preference isn't to rely heavily on maps, but if you'd rather plot out your route clearly to accommodate the needs of your body, I encourage you to do that! For instance, if you have a wheelchair or mobility device, it might be important for you to know what routes you'll be able to navigate with the most ease. If you have a health condition which requires frequent bathroom usage, it may be good to do that research ahead of time and learn where the public bathrooms on your route are. Whatever your access needs are, I encourage you to work with my ideas as a base and adapt it to whatever works for you and your body right now. You can still do this exercise and notice the vibes of where you are. Energy work is fun, but your safety and health should always come first. Sometimes I overestimate my walking stamina, and take an Uber or public transit home. Nothing wrong with it! Let this be an exercise in listening to your body and your environment.

Once you've done this exercise a few times and gotten to know the streets and pathways in your area, try to notice the shifts in vibe between different swaths of street. If you've been in your neighbourhood for quite some time, chances are you've already been doing this, without thinking too much about it: it's something many of us do subconsciously and intuitively. Do you have any favourite streets or homes or trees or creeks or corners in your neighbourhood? What resonates about the energy there? Take note, literally or in your mind.

If you're in an urban or suburban area, notice which houses or apartment buildings feel warm and cozy, which feel tense. How can you tell? Try not to base this on any exterior noticing. Making assumptions based on how well-kept or fancy a house looks doesn't mean you're practicing honing your energy skills. Feel into your body instead, with the different 'clair' skills listed earlier in this chapter. This process may help you notice which ways of sensing come to you with the most ease, and which are a little harder for you to access.

You may wish to record your observations, in a notebook, voice note, the notes app on your phone, or even just in your memory bank. When I write things down, it helps me remember where my skill level was. It's a lot easier to notice, measure, and appreciate my own progress when keeping records of what I've been up to and how I felt doing it. If you don't have the time to write down a novel after or during every walk, don't sweat it – start where you are. A simple list or series of five words can do the trick, and can be helpful in jogging our memory later. You never know what patterns and wisdom might emerge over time, once you revisit these notes.

INSTIGATING ENERGETIC SHIFTS

We don't do anything completely by ourselves, and what all of this work really is creation and manifestation, in collaboration with all that is – spiritual beings, the earth, ourselves, and everything in between.

What we're really doing on the ground is instigation; connecting with the catalyst that we can be and in fact always are. Our body is our first environment, and as we move about in the places we live and breathe and love in, it's important to know how to shift those spaces too, whether it's as simple as the energy in our human body or in our apartment, or as big and far reaching as shifting our neighborhood, city, and culture.

When we intentionally shift energy in our selves and our spaces, we create the groundwork for action. It's important to be aware of our energy, and that of the space we will be doing our spiritual work and ritual in, so that our body and any other environment we choose can act as an incubator, a workspace, a studio, a place of growth where boundaries can be safely and consensually pushed.

So, choose your space. Notice the state of energy in your body, and where you are. What now? Sit in the room by yourself, silently, with the lights off. Close your eyes and feel where you are. Let the room reveal itself to you. If you have difficulty focusing during silent meditation, try playing a guided meditation tape or repetitive rhythm, like that of a drum. Sound, especially repetitive sound, is a useful technique to enter an altered state of consciousness.

An altered state of consciousness is distinct from our ordinary consciousness; when we are in it, we may be more open to receiving messages from spirit and feeling the energy around us. This may be a light trance state, a 'flow' state familiar to athletes and artists, or even those who have a regular practice of increased relaxation, meditation, or prayer. There are many kinds of altered states, and even more ways to get there – but getting into these frames of mind can help us connect spiritually, especially if it's an area of ourselves we're trying to gain deeper access to. Experienced practitioners able to multitask often don't need to get into an altered state in order to feel energy and make spirit contact, and can simply do these things in ways that are seamlessly integrated into daily life.

Try to connect with the room's energy signature left by days, months, years of (potentially thoughtless) use. Listen to what these energies reveal to you. If your mind wanders and you find yourself thinking about dinner, let it pass, and peacefully return to your original line of thought.

Though in my descriptions I refer to indoor space, these exercises can easily be adapted for outdoor use. When working outdoors, however, we need to be especially mindful of the creatures and spirits who inhabit that environment. I really would recommend doing this in your indoor space – all spaces and places can instigate spiritual connectedness, not just the outdoors! Spiritual connection is possible where you are now – wherever that is. Busy coffee shop, skyscraper lunch break, or suburban backyard.

After you've felt out the space, and yourself, it's important to consider how you might cleanse and prepare the space for the work you will be doing, even if that's just simple day to day living! That counts! Whatever the work, it is important to engage the space where you are, and your body, with intention.

There is no one specific way to cleanse space. If you have any cultural or spiritual traditions that are meaningful to you, feel free to draw from those traditions when creating intentional space for yourself, whether for the purpose of work, ritual, and sustained growth.

Below, I describe a handful of different tried-and-true access points and methodologies for instigating energetic shift. I invite you to pick and choose what resonates with you, and adapt it to align with your own culture, circumstances, belief system, and worldview. With these techniques as a base, get inspired and be creative! Play, try new things—take note of what works for you and what doesn't.

SHIFTING BY VISUALIZING

Visualize a big glowing ball of light around yourself and the environment you're in. What color is it? What does it look like? Is it thick, thin? Blue? Pointy? Imagine that by envisioning it, it becomes reality. Think of qualities you would like the space to have. Would you like everyone in it to feel comfortable? Maybe you want a space that feels especially safe, like a big comfy bed in the wintertime. What other energetic qualities and vibes are important to you?

In this visualization, you can also prepare for any potential unwanted negative energies which may try to shatter the environment you're envisioning. One way to engage with this is to visualize dark tendrils of energy drifting towards your sphere; visualize them bouncing off and transforming from grey into white energy.

You can use any color that has positive associations for you, on a personal or cultural level. Though I do not personally hold white to always symbolize positive and constructive energy—and I'm aware of some cultures that associate white with evil, death, or nasty vibes in general—I am embedded within a Western framework and society that does hold these associations, where 'white' is associated with light and happiness and 'black' is associated with darkness and negativity. What candle color do most folks in Western magic traditions use for cleansing and healing? White. What about for banishing? Black.

With an awareness of this, when teaching others how to visualize energy, I usually keep with the black/white dichotomy of negative/positive, because the Western cultural associations with these colors can help strengthen the integrity of the visualization for those who are learning in a Western context. However, you can use any color that is meaningful to you. Sometimes, in order to break free of these cultural associations, I use pink and grey as examples instead—pink for health and peace, grey for anything nasty I want to get rid of. Maybe in your visualization, you'll use orange to represent a positive, loving, safe space. Maybe you'll use red to represent dangerous energy. The colors you choose are less important than the meanings you associate with each color.

Visualization is very personal, so don't get caught up on someone else's symbols! Use your own.

Personalize the technique so that it has more power and truth for you. If for you white symbolizes death and lack of health, and black represents power and peace, go with it!

SHIFTING BY SWEEPING

This is a technique I learned from my childhood in Spiritualism. We can cleanse the energies of ourselves and the spaces we inhabit by sweeping away any harmful vibes that we've picked up throughout the day. Some of us may like to do this with our bodies or hands, and some with tools or objects like brooms. Whichever way you're more comfortable with is fine!

In order to get rid of any harmful energies you've been carrying around, you can cleanse your body by hovering your hands about one to two inches above your body parts, and as you visualize any nasty vibes leaving you, sweeping your hands away from your body, and if necessary, making a flicking motion with your fingers (as though you had water on your hands and want to flick it at somebody), or a pulling motion, as if pulling a stray herb out of your cup of tea. As you visualize these negative energies leaving you, imagine them transforming into something positive. You may want to start with the top of your head, and move down to your face, your chest, each arm, and then down the rest of your body. In Spiritualism, I have heard this referred to as taking a dry shower— cleansing your body of any energies which have been causing you grief or dragging you down. If it helps to imagine this process as taking a shower, use the same gestures you would as if you were showering in water. Since we often shower to clean ourselves, rather than solely for personal enjoyment, the symbolism here can help us connect spiritually to the idea of an energetic and spiritual cleanse through a physical sweeping or showering motion.

You can use a broom to do this, as well, but in my practice I have found a broom is more useful for sweeping large spaces or rooms, rather than bodies, unless you have a very small broom! More tools are not always better, and can sometimes feel cumbersome or in the way. If you do choose to work with a broom, use the same visualization process as outlined above—as you sweep, imagine ridding the space of any psychic or energetic nasty vibes or 'dirt,' anything that does not serve you or your workings.

I don't intend to reify Victorian notions of cleanliness and purity, and the value judgments associated with that period of time which seem almost inescapable in today's world, with all this talk of 'cleansing' and 'dirt' in spiritual and wellness spaces. Instead, I am referring to that which is harmful and that which is helpful; that which inspires us and gives us strength, and that which weakens us, hurts us, and tempts us to give up. And I don't mean to suggest that there is no power in exploring darker shadow sides of life—there is much healing and wisdom to be found there. But, there's an important difference between exploring our shadow and engaging in self-abuse.

One way to think about the dichotomy created by the rhetoric of energetically transforming space and ourselves is to frame things in terms of that which serves us, and that which does not. Generally speaking, most people aim to become closer to what makes us happy and gives us joy and strength (even if these things are challenging or difficult, such as healing from abuse), and to distance ourselves from situations, energies, or choices which may hinder our efforts towards strength, peace, happiness, healing, personal and community growth, and causes we believe in. We can let go of abusive or unhelpful friends, lovers, and family members, habits, mindsets, stories.

SHIFTING WITH PLANTS

The search for appropriate herbs to use in magic and ritual doesn't need to begin with an encyclopedic book. An herb is not more meaningful, magical, or powerful if you can't pronounce its name or have never heard of it before. One way to approach working with plants is to consider what plants you interact with on a regular basis. What plants do you eat? Which plants nourish you? What plant beings do you work with in your cooking, or to decorate your home? Which plants are in your garden? Which plants do you know how to cultivate from seed? Which plants grow outside where you live, in public parks or local forests? Which plants push up through cracks in the pavement? The plants that are already interwoven into your life can be powerful allies, healers, and collaborators. These plants already share a connection with you, and so may be good choices as you begin this work. Maybe you live in Canada, like I do, where cedar, pine, and dandelion are everywhere. They have proven to be powerful allies to me. I've built a strong relationship with the mint plant by taking it as a tea for medicinal purposes, and I've come to know basil as a powerful protector by growing it on my windowsill.

Once you have a plant or two in mind, meditate with that plant. Connect with it, see what it tells you. After you do this is the time to look at herbal correspondence books and see what the plant's medical uses are and what the plant has historically been used for magically. If you are working in a public space, or somewhere that there are animals or children, I would advise against using any harmful plants. Poisonous plants have their own special and important uses, but noxious herbs are best left to the expertise of the seasoned practitioner. Whatever plants you're working with, be sure to consult medical herbal books if the plant is unfamiliar to you. We know many herbs and plants used in cooking are edible and safe to work with in lots of different ways, but other more obscure plants may not be. It's always worth double-checking, for the sake of everyone's safety. And some very common "witchy" herbs are toxic to cats and dogs, so be careful with what you're bringing into your home! Always do your research, and double-check your sources. It's best to trust works written by trained herbalists, doctors, or pharmacists.

One way to work with herbs to intentionally transform space is to sprinkle bits of the herb around the room. Or, you can tie some of the plants together with a string and hang them around the room, fresh or dried. If you are picking your own herbs or plants, be sure to harvest them with intention—ask for consent, don't overharvest, thank the plant, and leave an offering.

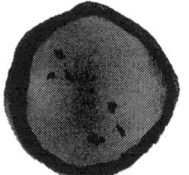

Shifting with Stones

Much of what is written above can also be applied to selecting stones. You may have a stone that means a lot to you. Maybe it's a quartz necklace, maybe it's a big chunk of amethyst on your dresser. Maybe it's a simple stone you picked up at your local park. Whatever it is, it can work with you to intentionally set up space. Use your intuition to select stones that call to you, that you feel may align with the kind of space you intend to create. You can also consult reference books for this if you wish.

Many practitioners recommend cleansing stones regularly, especially before collaboration to cleanse a space. You can do this by burying your stone underneath the earth, setting it outside on the night of a full moon, or even laying it in a dish of sea salt. Not so into those ideas? No problem – feel free to simply hold the stone between the palms of your hands and visualize. With each of these techniques, if you engage them with intention, the stone will absorb the energy of either the earth itself, or of the moonlight, or whatever you're visualizing, as a cleansing agent that can provide a bit of an energetic reset. Whatever techniques you use to transform the energy of a space or person can be enacted on stones as well.

Shifting energy by working with stones themselves is a very simple and low-key practice that can be easily adapted to situations where something more overtly "magical" might be seen as invasive or inappropriate. You can wear a gemstone necklace or other form of jewelry (in my years of practice, there have been times where I wore lots of gemstone rings, as well as turquoise jewelry in my navel and nostrils), put a small tumbled stone into the pocket of your jeans, or even carry around a small bag with a few favorite stones in it within your purse, briefcase, or backpack.

The idea here is that just by being in the proximity of a particular stone, its benefits will be absorbed into your own energy field. Feeling tired? You can carry around a stone to help energize you or act as a talisman. Just need some grounding energy to keep you down to earth? Select a stone known for this type of energy and spend some quality time with it, either actively (meditating with it, asking it to speak to you and recording any impressions) or passively (walking around with it in your back pocket). Do your best to learn about the stone and its journey to you; we'll talk more about the importance of this in a later chapter.

One caveat here with stones – I don't believe any being is disposable, and that includes gemstones harvested in violent and extractive ways. We can fight against unsustainable mining and violation of the earth while still embracing, loving, and working with the mineral beings we came into contact with. A full in-depth account of the politics and political economy of gemstone mining is outside the scope of this book, but I'd encourage you to do some research and check out where your witchy crystals come from, and how they make their way to you.

Something else to keep in mind is that gemstones have the highest profit margin of any good sold at most witchy, woo woo, spiritual, or new age shops – so there's often more at play when a shopkeeper tries to sell you a crystal for every mood or problem you may have. Crystals, minerals, and stones are all beautiful beings with personalities, energies, and abilities – but the way they're often spoken of is as quick-fix solutions, rather than as beings in their own right. Try to get to know these stones as they are, rather than as a simple means to an end. This is true for all beings, of course – but I've never seen the oversimplified 'buy this to feel better' sales technique anywhere so often as I have with gemstones.

Shifting with Sound

Ring some bells or clap your hands to clear the room of any nasty energies. You can also play music—and this doesn't have to be hippie new-age music, either. It can be contemporary or old school, anything that makes you feel good and want to dance. It can even be something that makes you feel calm and relaxed (or pumped up, if that's what you're going for). As long as the music makes you feel good and gives you good energy, play it! The specifics of what you play are less important than how the music makes you feel. Pick music that inspires the kind of feeling you want to permeate your working space and in your body. This may change based on what kind of work you're doing. For instance, to connect with healing energy, the music you choose may be very different than the music played to set the space for a ritual to banish bad habits. Sometimes angry, sad music may be exactly what a ritual needs.

Shifting with Movement

Many of us need music to dance—so if you decide to play music, don't be afraid to move around! Even if you're doing this by yourself, play some songs and dance, move, sway, stomp your feet and move your arms. No one's watching, so get that energy out! As long as you dance and move with intention, all of the energy you expend dancing will go towards shifting energies in your space and in your body. My apartment's secret name is basically Rap Music Dance Party With Cats, so please allow yourself to be inspired and fearless. This is about you, so it doesn't matter if you look silly or uncoordinated. Movement – in this case – is not about how you look, it's about how you feel, and the energetic change that movement inspires in you, your body, your space, and your environment.

If dancing isn't quite right for you, that's ok too. Roll, spin, stretch. You can even move about and jiggle while seated or lying down, if mobility is a challenge or concern for you, or if you're just not in the mood today. Listen to your body.

SHIFTING WITH LIGHT

When do you feel best? With bright lights, or with the lights dim and moody? Personally, I prefer sunlight accented by candlelight during the daytime, and dim lights with candles once the sun has set. Flame is always an important aspect of lighting for me, but if you'd rather work with tinted lightbulbs and electricity for safety, financial, or other reasons, that's perfectly fine! Some folks I know have lights that they can program with their phones, in order to create interesting color combinations and vibes, without actually incorporating fire.

If this is something you're interested in as a way of shifting space, do some research and experiment. Light is a huge contributor to mood and can drastically change the energy in a space and in our bodies. For instance, fluorescent lights, especially when flickering, always trigger migraines and nausea for me, so I need to be careful and aware of the lighting wherever I am. However, I know someone who loves white fluorescent light, and hates my favourite 'mood' lighting – everyone's different!

A quick note on candles: Fire is something to be careful with. You don't want to burn down your indoor space, and you don't want to risk starting a forest fire if you're working outdoors. If this is something you're worried about, you might want to consider using candles encased in glass. The bonus in using these candles is that the wax is contained within the glass, and you won't have to clean it up off the carpet or iron it out of fabric like you would when unencased candles drip drop everywhere. Another benefit of glass jar candles is your companion animals won't accidentally set their tails on fire as they walk past – I've actually had this happen! (Everyone was safe, my cat didn't even notice – the fire went out immediately with the next wave of her tail, and she had no idea why I was freaking out! Since then, I almost exclusively work with jar candles.)

Another benefit of glass jar candles is that you can draw, paint, or paste on the glass with a marker some key words you want to summon into your environment. You could also draw pictures or designs that represent those feelings to you – and have a visual representation of it while you're setting up and establishing the space. Be careful, though, and do keep an eye on them. I've had glass jar candles crack, shatter, and break during particularly powerful workings.

SHIFTING WITH SMOKE

Smoke cleansing is usually done by setting dried herbs or plants on fire. Blow out the flame, or wave the herb around. This can either be a stick or cone of incense, a bundle of dried herbs, or crushed dried herbs with resin on charcoal; and the herb or incense will usually continue to smoke until much of the plant material has burned up. You may have to put it out early, by snuffing it out in a mini iron cauldron or similar, or you may have to re-light it. If you're working indoors, try to open as many windows as you can. I've never had an issue with smoke cleansing and smoke detectors, but your mileage may vary.

Move around the space with your burning herbs, and imagine the energies of the herb mixing with your environment, transforming it into the kind of space you would like it to be. As you walk around the room, think of the qualities you'd like your space (and your body!) to radiate—maybe safety, love, strength, confidence, softness. Or maybe you're looking for something more challenging, and if that's the case, walk the smoke around the room with the intention that it become a safe container for working through concerns and thoughts which may be difficult or uncomfortable, but ultimately necessary and important.

The Magic of Self-Care

Whenever I talk with most people about energetic work and why it's important, I usually tell the same story.

It happened in one of my favorite classes when I was in undergrad. One day, a guest came and spoke about the pain and turmoil faced by their community. After the presentation, I reached into my bag to grab the tea I had prepared before leaving my house and was met by the unpleasant sound of creaking glass—my insulated glass thermos had shattered, leaving shards of glass littered all over the interior of my knapsack.

I went on to speak with some other friends who had attended class and they all complained of headaches and exhaustion. This was attributed to the energy of the guest speaker and the pain they had carried with them into the classroom. I was thankful to hear the guest's story, and remain certain that they had no idea of the energetic impact they had on the classroom – all the more reason to learn about energy work, as often when people can't control their own energy (be it coming from a place of trauma, anger, etc), they can leave an impact that is not always intentional.

Next time I saw my classmates I asked them how they were, and apparently it had taken each of them a few days to recover from that energetic whiplash. I, however, felt fine and had no recovery to speak of, and indeed nothing to recover from.

Why was this? Because I maintain a healthy energetic self-care practice. My classmates didn't—and felt the burn from that. What they were doing was the energetic equivalent of not wearing a rain jacket in a thunderstorm—of course they got soaked! I was wearing one (so to speak), so it makes complete sense that I kept dry. In class, I had shielded myself, but I forgot to shield my bag. As a result, the guest speaker's energy hit my bag, and shattered my glass bottle. This was a physical reminder of the potency and power of energy—it can cause illness in people, and actually break objects.

A decade ago, I was in Halifax doing an artist residency. I love to shop when I travel, and one day I stopped by a boutique to pick up some clothes I'd put on hold. It was a bit of an upscale place with a spiritually conscious vibe and as I waited in line I heard the gentleman in front of me talk about how he felt so overwhelmed all the time because he is 'so sensitive' to energy. It sounded a bit more like bragging than a genuine complaint. I had so much to say, but held my tongue.

There is a weird romanticization where people think that being spiritually and energetically sensitive to the extent that they are in pain or discomfort is exotic and cool, that it makes them special and deserving of praise and sympathy. While being naturally energetically sensitive is a great and powerful gift, all of us can get there with time and practice if we want to.

However, in my mind these complain-brags always have an undercurrent of 'I have no idea what I am doing.' The reason people get overwhelmed by energy on a daily basis and get thrown off by even the most basic energetic stuff is most likely because they have no energetic self-care practices, or at least none that are sufficiently effective. Of course, we can all get overwhelmed and tired, and we all let our guard down sometimes—this happens to me too! That being said, the glorification of bad spiritual self-care doesn't help any of us stay safe and protect our energy.

There are some things that it is beneficial to be aware of if you want to have a healthy energetic self-care practice. Energetic self-care is a really good place to start if you're trying to get your feet wet and slowly become accustomed to working with magic and witchcraft.

I encourage you to begin to cultivate an awareness of the differences between days or situations when you do and don't use the following techniques. Do you notice any differences in your bodily sensations, your emotions, your mental state?

It may help to take notes as you go, so you can compare how you feel throughout the journey of practicing these techniques.

Grounding Energy

Grounding energy is a very important thing to know how to do! Sometimes when people are really energetically sensitive, they can get headaches or become dizzy—I've seen this happen to magical practitioners in ritual, and to sensitive folks who don't have an intentional energy practice. A grounding practice consists of becoming rooted and stable; it can be equalizing. It's possible to have too much earthy energy, and in those instances you're not grounded and stable but sluggish and tired in a way that is unhealthy, unpleasant, or undesired—so you need to get rid of it. Likewise, grounding can also be about bringing too much airy scattered energy back down to earth.

Grounding may be helpful when you feel agitated, overwhelmed, dizzy, depressed. Think of it as a stabilizer. For me, the basis of grounding is in the breath. If you have a yoga practice or engage in energy healing work, this process will be familiar to you. If you jive with tree symbolism, imagine your feet extending down into the ground and growing roots, like a big strong tree, unwavering, stable, calm, confident, capable. You may want to inhale strength and rootedness, exhale agitation, anxiety, nervousness.

Grounding can also be as simple as getting some food in your belly, or getting in touch with your physicality (for instance, through sitting outside under a tree, lying in bed with a book, doing yoga or stretching, etc).

Going Deeper

Cultivating an awareness of energy is incomplete without adequate knowledge on how to ground excess energies we can encounter when performing ritual work. If not well grounded or shielded, new practitioners may feel ill after magical practice. Their body may not know how to deal with excess energy, and so they may get headaches, feel dizzy, sick to their stomachs, or pass out from overexertion.

Notice that none of the energy shifting techniques discussed in this chapter involve expending one's personal energy. Instead, the methods involve awareness and shifting of energies surrounding us—such as energies from candlelight, herbs, the earth, sunshine, rain clouds, and everything in between. We can work with energy as a channel or conduit, rather than expending all of our own.

It's important to look after our health and well-being as magical practitioners. If you feel exhausted after a magical working, there's a big chance that there's something seriously wrong with your technique, or at least that there could stand a little improvement in there somewhere – for your own well being!

In Western traditions, often the four Greek elements of earth, air, fire, and water are cited as some of the energetic building blocks of magic. So, since that is the place I speak from and work within, the suggestions I offer for grounding will scaffold upon these elements.

As with everything written in this book, feel free to modify and adapt the techniques I outline to be more in alignment with your specific personal and cultural frame of reference. There are many different elemental frameworks across cultures.

GROUNDING WITH AIR

Light some incense and let the smoke surround you, perfuming your space. Breathe in the scent, and wear it like a shroud that calms and comforts you. If you aren't into smoke for whatever reason, an alternative is to use an oil burner. Be sure to choose a scent that calms you and helps you get rid of any excess energies. If you're sensitive to artificial fragrance and chemicals, be careful what you purchase, and do your best to ensure what you have comes directly from plant matter. If you have a sensitive nose, you'll be able to smell the difference. I recommend against buying anything without a clear ingredients list.

GROUNDING WITH FIRE

After a ritual, it may be helpful to light some candles. I know if I'm having an intense day and have too much pent-up energy, surrounding myself with candles calms me down and keeps me in a peaceful, relaxed frame of mind. If you live in a home with a fireplace, you might want to curl up in front of the fire. Or, if you're like me and live in a small downtown apartment, you can sit in front of your space heater, or with your heating pad. Focusing on the sensations of warmth can be incredibly soothing, and can help dissipate any excess energy that may still be with you after magic work. As you savor the warmth emanating from your choice of heat source, visualize all excess energy leaving your body and flowing down beneath your feet. If you live somewhere sunny and opt for a morning ritual, you can also just go lie outside in a nearby park and soak up the sunshine. Practice feeling cozy, warm, and held by the heat.

GROUNDING WITH WATER

After you finish doing any kind of heavy energy work, it can be helpful to take a shower. Baths also work very well, but if you're going to go that route, I still suggest taking a shower afterwards if you can. As you feel drops of water beating against your skin, imagine all excess and built-up energy leaving your body, washed away by fresh clean water (or, if you're taking a bath, imagine it seeping from your pores, into the water, and down the drain). Be sure not to get rid of too much energy, though, or make the water too too hot—you want to feel grounded and strong, not weak and wiped out. Focus on feeling centered, at peace, stable, comfortable.

Also: tea. For many people, a hot tea herbal infusion can be an incredibly stabilizing way to ground with water. You may already have a regular relationship to tea, and perhaps even wind down with your own ritual of drinking some tea after dinner, or in the morning when you wake up. Be sure to select something that's going to help your battery feel full – something both calming and energizing might be good to try.

Some of my favourite herbs to work with in tea form are holy basil, peppermint, rose, and ginger. Note that the form a plant takes will impact the time it needs to stay immersed in hot water. Flower petals need the least time, dried herbs need a little more, and a root like ginger requires at least forty minutes in boiling water. Whichever plants you choose, as you feel the hot liquid travel through your digestive system, imagine its warmth grounding and stabilizing you from the inside out.

GROUNDING WITH EARTH

One way to ground yourself with earth after a ritual or energy work is to eat! This is probably my favorite way to ground. The grounded feeling eating can give us is exactly what you want after an intense ritual! No one wants or needs residual energy making us feel scattered and staying with us after we leave a ritual.

For a communal ritual, the most fun way to do this may be to have a potluck! Ask every participant to bring a dish for everyone to share and enjoy together after the ritual. (As an aside, I suggest making ingredients lists mandatory—those with special diets, allergies, and food sensitivities will thank you.) If you're doing a public outdoor working, and the weather permits, you can always plan a group picnic after the work is complete. If the ritual was difficult or serious, this is also a great way to regroup and debrief with delicious food and friendly conversation.

You can also spend time outdoors, lying in the grass, or with your back against a big tree. Go outside, take a walk, feel your feet make contact with the earth. Vibe with that connection and focus on feeling held and stable. If going outside and spending time with the local flora isn't an option, you might wish to try meditating while holding a stone or plant of your choice. Maybe you have a quartz necklace that always anchors you when you wear it, or a pouch of dried herbs you collected on your last hike. Try sitting with the item and connecting with its energy.

Whatever it is you choose to help you ground, be sure it is something that you associate calm, solid, grounding vibes with. When grounding, you should avoid any objects whose energy signatures cause you to feel agitated, worried, nervous, stressed, or excited.

GROUNDING WITH SPIRIT

You can lead yourself through a visualization to ground excess energy, as a way of connecting with spirit. Whichever techniques you feel drawn to, you will have to contend with visualization along the way at some point; in this work, it is unavoidable. It's also a more difficult way of engaging with energy —a lot of practitioners, particularly newer practitioners, like the visual aids, the ritual theatre of constantly working with 'witchy' objects, or the incorporation of anything with a 'mystical' association into their work.

Since it's likely that you won't always have helpful physical grounding aids on hand, it's important to know how to ground without them! This way, you don't become too reliant on external objects as crutches for your energy work.

If you're feeling sick from energy overload and you can only ground yourself effectively with your lucky amethyst, your health and vibe may be compromised; you may feel discomfort and pain longer than you would if you had honed your visualization skills to ground yourself in preparation for the unlucky day when you left your amethyst at home. When we cultivate our skills in working with our own bodies and minds, we can access magic wherever we are, no matter what's going on – and support ourselves through it.

One way to accomplish this is to imagine roots extending down from beneath your feet, into the earth beneath you. Then, visualize all excess energy (be it agitation, nervousness, headaches, dizziness) trickling down into the ground, into the earth, into the soil, beneath the concrete or grass where you are. Feel the rootedness of your body, embedded in the ground like a tree—trunk strong and sturdy, roots deep. After a few minutes of reinforcing this visualization you should feel grounded and refreshed. Continue until you begin to feel at least a little different! If you don't resonate with a tree visualization, you can also curl up into a ball and imagine yourself as a stone or a rock. I've seen this work very well with young children whose energy levels are over the top!

If neither of those images resonate with you, feel free to switch them out for something that does. Be creative and give yourself permission to explore.

SHEILDING ENERGY

This is probably my favorite (and the most important) technique I'll talk about here. If you consider yourself really empathetic, sympathetic, energetically sensitive (or oversensitive), and if you find yourself in a constant barrage of spirit contact, or the excessive energies coming from other people, this will be of particular use to you—but all folks can and should embrace shielding if it feels resonant. It's basic energetic protection.

If shielding seems odd to you and you'd rather not do it, that's entirely up to you, but I recommend exploring at least some kind of regular energetic protection and boundary work. In order to live healthy, balanced lives, it can be helpful to know how to have some control over our energetic sensitivity and connection to spirit(s), to be able to turn our skills on and off, to cultivate some agency in regard to how we are impacted by what goes on around us.

There are many different ways to shield. A good way to begin is by visualizing a sphere around yourself. This can be a glowing light and may be any color depending on what associations you have with different colors and what you are trying to achieve with your shield.

You can do something general for protection, or something that keeps you safe and also heals you, or you can shield yourself from specific people or entities—or all of the above at once! Focus your intention on what your goal is—shields are entirely programmable and have a lot to do with your specific needs.

Here's an example: Let's say I want to do a simple shield against harmful vibes, which also rids me of any energetic nasties that have latched onto me. I might visualize myself enveloped in a thick glowing egg of white light. I could then envision any harmful energy that I am holding onto in grey, and visualize it dissipating as my shield becomes stronger. Something else I could do is picture grey nasty vibes coming at me and bouncing off the shield, transforming from grey into white energy. If you are going to visualize nasty energy moving away from you, be sure to visualize it changing into positive energy that is healing, nourishing, and stabilizing.

Another reason to shift the bad vibes around you is that you don't want to wade around in yucky energy! What good is a shield if you're still surrounded by and wading through the crap you just banished?

You can layer your shield, too, if you like—make a layer that looks like leaves, or maybe a giant bubble, or something that's constantly moving like flames. Or, perhaps there's a gemstone you deeply identify with and see as a protective ally. Imagine one layer of your shield taking on that shape and color. The exact specifics of what it is matters less than what that thing means to you. If you have a special connection with the wind and feel that element is an especially meaningful and powerful spiritual ally for you, you can imagine a sphere of wind as your shield. The baggage of associations matter here. Try out different types of shields, and take note on what works best for you, and what's more and less effective.

When you're learning and trying out this stuff you may want to sit in a quiet room with a candle and some incense so you can really focus on what you're doing and notice the new sensations in your body and mind that go along with this energetic practice.

However, it's important to remember that you won't always have access to a silent room with dim lights and an aromatherapy candle to calm your nerves. You may be in a situation where people surround you, or where everything is a bit chaotic, like on a bus or walking through crowded streets, when you need to practice shielding energy. If it helps, you may want to spend a minute in a bathroom where you know you will have complete privacy to focus on the energetic work uninterrupted.

Once you get used to it, you'll be able to effectively shield in any situation with ease, despite how stressful or agitating your environment is. If you're really sensitive and feel energetically exhausted after you go out dancing or walking the streets due to other peoples' psychic baggage, shielding is especially important to do often! Try it – I promise it'll help.

Another form of shielding is the 'don't fuck with me' aura. This works by shifting what your energetic field is doing. It can—if you want it to—function as an invisibility cloak of sorts, too. It just depends on how you program it and what kind of energy you are putting out. You can rouse up emotions or intentions in your self, mind, body, and energy field to express a specific type of vibe to yield certain results. At night I usually opt for 'don't fuck with me' rather than invisibility, because that's more my style and in alignment with how my energy is and how I move in the world, but as with much of this stuff, that choice is yours to make. Experiment with multiple options, and see which works best for you in different situations. Of course, don't forget normal safety precautions.

CLEANSING

Most of us cleanse on the regular by showering or taking a bath. This can be a magical act without much effort; intention, as always, is paramount here. Next time you're showering, visualize the water washing away any lingering negativity or pain from the day. You can be more specific, of course!

If you'd like to use your body in a different way to achieve cleansing, you can use the same visualization and intention when washing dishes by hand. As you scrub each dish, with each motion imagine what you wish to cleanse washing away down the drain. As the dishes become clean, you become cleansed. You can scrub away whatever you like: keep it generic and scrub away what no longer serves you, or be specific and wipe away any feelings that have lingered a bit too long, perhaps about an ex-partner or friends who are no longer in your life.

It's worthwhile to cleanse regularly. There's usually stuff we carry around without realizing how much it's truly impacting us. A great time to check in with yourself about this is just after the full moon, as it begins to wane or get smaller. As the moon gets smaller, it's most aligned with cleansing and banishing work. Can't wait til the next moon phase? No problem – the sun wanes, too!

Earlier in this chapter, I discuss one energetic cleansing technique, the dry shower (Shifting with Sweeping). Truly, most energetic shift techniques in this chapter can also be used to cleanse yourself (your body, mind, spirit), any space or physical environment, or an object of your choice. These methods are very versatile.

A cleanse is an energetic shift, of course, but the desired outcome here is to remove, dissipate, or neutralize something that may be harmful to us if it lingers on. Regular cleansing is an important part of energetic and magical hygiene—but don't worry, even I sometimes forget the importance of keeping it up and need to remind myself from time to time. So, if you forget, don't worry – you can pick it back up again any time.

When learning these techniques, I think it is useful to start with our own body as a barometer—then, once we feel the differences and changes in ourselves, we'll have a similar sensory apparatus in place when it's time to cleanse our apartment, home, classroom, or wherever!

We might want to cleanse ourselves to remove bad feelings that originate either outside of us or, as is often the case, within us. I'm a big fan of working through things rather than endlessly avoiding them, and spiritual bypassing is both a massive waste of time and far too rampant within witchy communities these days.

If you're not sure what the term 'spiritual bypassing' means, the very short version is that it involves using spiritual philosophies and ideas in order to 'bypass' rather than work through difficult feelings.

Of course, we all want to feel good rather than terrible, and working with spiritual tools to help us maintain a positive mindset never hurts – but/and, sometimes this can be taken to a bit of an extreme, where tough emotions are avoided at all costs, and often to the detriment of ourselves and our relationships. The phrase 'good vibes only,' visible on many a dating profile, is one example of this – and is even sometimes considered a form of gaslighting, minimizing questions or concerns around
complaint and/or discomfort, especially in spiritual communities.

However, sometimes we may just want to cleanse ourselves of anxiety before we go out on a date, or before a big presentation. Calming our nerves is very different from spiritual bypassing, and there's no problem with using magical techniques to make our lives a little easier, and to support us in our growth, strength, and healing.

Chapter Three

Magic and You

MAGIC AS COLLABORATION

Some critics of solitary witchcraft practitioners argue that you can't be a witch alone.
And I actually agree with this! But... not in the way you might think.

Witchcraft is always already collaborative. Even if we're standing by ourselves in front of our altar – maybe with a cat or two in the other room, maybe with incense swirling, candles lit, some mood music, a paper and pencil to write down our intentions – we're not alone. We never are. We're always surrounded by other beings. Yes, to me, hanging out with a piece of paper and pencil and incense and all that means we're engaged in collaborative work. Our body is interacting with other bodies, our being is meeting and sharing space with other beings.

Within my own worldview – and this is a part of what makes my approach to magic a little unique – I don't see typical magical collaborators like candles or incense as inert objects to be 'used' for our own purposes in spellwork or ritual. No! The type of magic I practice aims to not be extractive (or, at least, not thoughtlessly so; after all, this life involves some unavoidable elements of give and take), and a crucial aspect of this philosophy and worldview involves noticing all beings as beings with their own subjectivities and personhoods, no matter how similar or dissimilar they seem to what I know of my own human existence and experience. Jane Bennett, in her book *Vibrant Matter*, talks about how anthropomorphism can work to displace anthropocentrism (due to its invitation to consider that the nnonhuman being might have as vivid a world and experience as we can – what a phenomenal basis in which to ground our lives, movements, and ethics, and it's with this awareness and intellectual framing that I think with the term 'body' here when referring to pretty much anything, even beings who most folks refer to as just 'objects.'

I won't be getting into my whole philosophy and the full-on specifics of my ontology here – you can read all about that in my first book, *Witchbody*!

Regardless of the specificities, the acknowledgement of magic and witchcraft as intentionally collaborative processes are foundational to everything else I will share in this chapter (and, really, this book)! If you're committed to seeing witchcraft as just you as the sole agential being acting upon an inert ground in order to suck what you desire out of existence, I suggest you might want to put this book down and consider another book on witchcraft.

Or, if you'd like to challenge yourself to open up your worldview – maybe you're feeling a little open to what I'm saying here, or at least curious about it – or maybe you're sitting there with your internal voice screaming, Oh my god, this is what I've always known and felt! – keep reading.

Magic as I do it and teach it and feel it is all about relationships. The success of our magic hinges on how strong our relationships are with the beings with whom we share community. For me, that's my bed, my blankets, lamps, altar space, saint statues, rosaries, lighter, countless candles, herbs, and incense, as well as the offerings of flowers, water, alcohol, and food I give. We're always in relationship all the time, even when we're not doing magic or witchcraft, even when we're just in our bedroom chilling out reading a book with a cat on our lap. Magic isn't about bribery – at least not the type of magic I teach. Magic isn't about giving gifts or offerings because we think that'll make Spirit A like us enough to go and do the thing.

Magic is about sustaining relationships – friendships, mentorships, devotional relationships – over time, paying homage to these beings, treating them respectfully regardless of whether or not it's 'magic time.' What I love about magic – and this is a big part of what I talk about in *Witchbody* – is that magic, for those who haven't yet noticed the wondrousness and vibrant vitality of all beings, can help draw the attention to how our life is already intertwined with so many both within us and outside of us, who we support and who supports us.

Magic is here, now, all around us, always.

Connecting with Yourself

So, okay, yes – magic is all about relationships, and relationship building – noticing the wondrous agency and speech and lives and influence of so many nonhuman bodies with whom we are in continuous interaction and flow. But. And.

It's also so, so crucial to be in deep, meaningful, loving relationship with yourself.

This can help our magic be better, stronger, more effective – and can help us connect with magic and our spiritual collaborators from a place of groundedness and inner strength and self awareness, rather than from a place of lack, desperation, and hopelessness.

Don't get me wrong – I've been in those deep, dark places as well. Sometimes I still have my bad days. With the rise of social media and the internet, it can be really easy to spend a lot of time focusing on others: what other people are doing, what other people are saying, what they're creating, who they're talking to, what they're buying, and… need I go on? I think you know what I'm talking about! And, unfortunately, with this increased sharing, can also come increased distraction, increased calling out, increased telling other people what's wrong with them, rather than simply focusing on ourselves. A preoccupation with what other folks are doing and saying – and the urge to reach out and curb or control them – can often come from our own personal sense of powerlessness, a feeling of ineffectiveness in our own lives.

I've had phases like that, too, trust me, so I'm not judging! That was me at seventeen, angry at everyone on the internet all the time. I think we all go through it – confusion, overwhelm, and maybe some shame about ourselves and where we're at in life, maybe even jealousy of someone in our sphere who has achieved something we desire for ourselves but haven't gotten yet. And so maybe we lash out, even just inside our heads – fuck that person! They suck for these reasons! The internet is, unfortunately, a cesspool of folks taking out their displeasure with themselves and their own lives on other people, many of whom they don't even know. In the spiritual community this behaviour is rife.

And these insecurities are expressed in the types of magic people do, too. Instead of doing magic to manipulate other people to our whims and desires, it's possible to do magic to transform ourselves into who we want to be – controlling and shaping ourselves, not others – and growing in the process.

The world can be a better place, a kinder place, a more collaborative place, the more internal work and self-reflection each of us does. Have you heard the phrase, people go to therapy to deal with people who don't go to therapy? It's true! And while talk therapy may not be immediately accessible to all of us, we can all intentionally engage in practices of stepping back, looking and feeling into ourselves, and reflecting on our past, our history, our traumas, our motivations, our limiting beliefs, our deepest desires, goals, and visions for ourselves. We can look at our patterns, how we've been acting. We can compare that to how we want to be, how we want to feel, how we want to act.

Oftentimes, the desire to overly control and fuck with other people, and to tear them down, comes from an unhappiness in ourselves. Magic – as a part of a system of many self-care and self-healing modalities, both allopathic, naturopathic, and otherwise – can help, but only insofar as we take up the challenge of truly meeting ourselves.

Really, really meeting ourselves.

Knowing ourselves better – including a sober assessment of our skills and… less fun parts – helps us select magical practices that are more effective and appropriate to where we're at and where we want to go, treating the cause of a problem, not just the symptom.

WHO ARE YOU?

This may seem like an obvious or flippant question, but it isn't – it's something I take super seriously, and encourage everyone I work with to take seriously.

When I ask this question to you today in this book, I'm not just asking about your identity markers, like race, gender, sexuality, class, body size and shape, or how you may be differently abled than what society takes to be the presumptive standard. Parts of your identity may have taken you a while to accept and/or grow into – and maybe you're still on a journey into figuring out who you are, and how you relate to various aspects of your identity, and how these characteristics impact both how you are received in the world, and how you receive the world.

If there are parts of yourself you struggle to accept and celebrate, I think many of us have been there – it's a common experience! Spirituality can be one of many places we lean into, explore, and discover who we are, and can really help us to move through moments of insecurity and uncertainty. Of course, you may wish to explore aspects of your multifaceted identity through spirituality.

Identity markers are important, and shouldn't be ignored – but/and, I do find sometimes simply having a particular identity marker – whether it is from a more privileged or marginalized group – can be a fast-track to being right, or being taken seriously, regardless of the merit of what we are saying. Power has different articulations in different contexts, and these things aren't always so cut and dry.

People of any identity – rich, poor, white, black, disabled, abled, fat, skinny, trans, cis, queer, straight, whatever – can be shitty, nasty, vindictive people. And people of any background can be good, kind, inquisitive, generous people. People of any background can be assholes, manipulative; people of any background can mobilize their identities in violent ways and guilt trip others.

Unfortunately, that old adage is true: hurt people hurt people.

In my teenage quest to find community and belonging, I fell into social justice communities, queer and trans communities, and survivor communities. It felt good to be around fellow queer and trans people. It felt affirming. It felt good to be around other survivors of abuse and rape – I felt like these people understood me, heard and affirmed my story of who I was and where I'd been, when so many others wouldn't or couldn't hear me or make space for the bigness of my pain.

Now that I'm in my thirties, becoming involved in those communities is the only almost regret I have in life. Yes, they heard and affirmed me in my trauma – but/and, this community did more violence unto my being than the 'straight' world ever did. My experience in these identity-based community spaces fucked me up, and it's taken a long time to address those harms to my psyche and concept of myself. These niche communities can at times be authoritarian, cultlike, and totalist, and can exacerbate or even create psychological wounds.

Affinity groups based on identity can be beautiful, and do have their own place, but sometimes we have to come out of them to really begin to see ourselves. I've come to see these identity-based groups as a bit of what writer Kurt Vonnegut would call a granfalloon – a 'proud and meaningless collection of human beings.'

What's the point of me talking about all this stuff on groups and identity in a section about finding out who you are? Well, sometimes identity groups, while well-intentioned and offering many benefits such as community and kinship, can sometimes take us further away from ourselves. This was definitely the case for me, and it took me years to realize this, and even more years to heal, and come meet myself anew, to discover my core.

Sometimes, when our identity is marginalized in the society in which we live, we might reach out to communities or groups in order to affirm us, and help us feel accepted and less alone. Social ties, after all, are essential for survival. Sometimes this can go really well and be healing in and of itself, and sometimes it can be really twisted, manipulative, dysfunctional, and violent.

Who are you at your core? What are your beliefs and values?

How do you treat other people, and how do you prefer to be treated?

How do you see other people? Do you flatten them based on your own assumptions about 'people like them,' or are you curious and open? What evidence do you have to support any assumptions you may have?

When you feel uncomfortable and/or triggered, do you lash out at other people? Or do you self-reflect, and realize that sometimes maybe your response isn't actually about what's going on in the present moment, but you've redirected a rage about something from your past into the person in front of you? This may not be the case all the time, of course, but I've seen it happen more often than not.

Do you have ideas that limit you – such as whether or not it'll ever be possible for you to find love, or be happy, or have fulfilling work?

Do you have a good idea of what your strengths and weaknesses are – both interpersonally, and professionally? How do you react when someone tells you about your skills and strengths? Are you able to take it in and integrate it into your conception of yourself, or do you avoid compliments at all costs?

How do you react when someone tells you that you messed up, hurt their feelings, or that there's something you can improve on? Do you get defensive and lash out, or do you collapse in shame? Or, do you take a step back and find whether or not you agree with them? Can you stand in your truth, whatever side that ends up falling on?

All of this is incredibly important when we think about, reflect on, and feel into who we are.

It impacts our magic, it impacts our spirituality – both how we do it, and what we aim to get out of it. A grounded, self-aware person is a grounded, self-aware witch, capaable of doing grounded, self-aware magic.

WHERE ARE YOU NOW?

So, with all that said, with all you've been through – the good and the bad and everything in between – where have you ended up? What have you created for yourself, for your life, with raw materials? What form have you shaped chaos into?

What do you need? What are you looking for?

Are you in therapy? (I think everyone should go to therapy.) Do you have a naturopath? Do you take multivitamins? Do you get enough sleep? Are you happy with your love life, your friendships, your career, your job? Do you adore where you live, or is it good enough for now?

Magic is so much about where we want to be – so much to the extent that many books and teachers on magic de-emphasize the now; in my opinion, often to the detriment of the student of magic.

Witchcraft works best when we support our spiritual and magical efforts with 'mundane world' efforts – these boring things you probably have heard about before, that maybe you or others think you 'should' do in order to get right with yourself and meet yourself more deeply than you are. Or maybe you're good – I don't know! I just know that for me, this will be a lifelong journey, a process I'll always be going through. And I love that.

This journey, for me, isn't motivated by discontentedness, but the desire to expand, to challenge myself, to see how much more I can be, how much more I can do, how much more fully I can live life, how much more fully I can feel. But that's me – maybe your journey, your expansion, is about becoming more insular, becoming more still. That's cool.

With this section, I'm mostly asking – when you look at yourself, feel yourself, notice yourself, sit with yourself, right now, what do you see? What of yourself is your base? What are your weak spots? What can you see? What can't you?

I'm thinking here with two key concepts – Donna Haraway's situated knowledges, and Sara Ahmed's concept of orientation. Orientation and situatedness might seem like two ways of talking about the same thing, and in some ways this may be true, but ultimately the nuance between and within these ideas is important.

WHERE HAVE YOU BEEN?

What has made you who you are?
What journeys have you been on?
What heartbreaks have you suffered?
What success have you experienced?
What have been your life peaks, your greatest joys?
What traumas have you experienced?
Have you talked about it?
Who hurt you?
Who have you hurt?
What did you do about it?
What loves have you had? How did you lose them? Who is still with you?
Where have you traveled? What books have you read?
What art have you made?

How many hills have you rolled down? How much fresh snow have you stomped through? How big were the puddles you splashed?

Who has held you? Who have you held?

Have you had any long dark nights of the soul? What started it? How did you emerge? What did you learn? How did you feel? What did you do next?

Have you had a Saturn Return yet? Are you in one now? Did you just exist, are you existing, did you learn the lessons, did you take the medicine, even if it tasted gross?

Have you been to therapy? What kind? How did it go? Are you still there? Do you need to go again?

Have you bled? Have you fallen apart? Have you sewn yourself back up? Did you get help?

Have you apologized?
Have you raged?
What feelings have you felt?
Have you cried?

Have you written wishes on slips of paper, released them into the ocean, into the lake, into the forest, into the air?

Have you felt so much joy that you felt your cheeks might burst? Have you laughed so hard you were covered in tears?

What have you never told anyone?
What shames have you felt?
What secrets do you still carry?

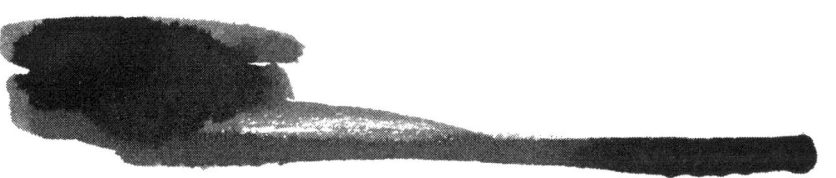

SITUATED AND ORIENTED

One of Haraway's key points on situated knowledges is that there is no 'view from nowhere.' We are all situated somewhere, and are thus viewing, knowing, creating, speaking from somewhere in particular.

This 'somewhere' is the cumulative effect of our experiences, our subject position, our identity and the experiences we've had as a result, where we've been and where we are. All of us is encapsulated into this idea of 'situated' – we are all marked, touched, by our experiences, our heritage, the harms we've experienced, the healing we've been blessed with or earned. None of us is speaking or doing or being 'from nowhere.' We were born somewhere and sometime, we are made up of genetic material from other people. We have roots, origins, lineages, positionalities.

We all bring with us our experiences, wherever we are – and this is true, too, in magic. Where we've been and where we are, our situatedness, shapes what and how we see the magical path before us.

Okay, so how does orientedness fit into this? Well, instead of being just about being situated in space in a particular position, orientendess reminds us that no matter where we're situated, we don't have all seeing eyes – there are certain things we're oriented towards, which are in our line of vision due to who we are and the experiences we've had – as well as things we're oriented away from, things we can't see due to our positionality and identity and life experiences. Orientedness helps explain so much – specialization and expertise in terms of vocation and education, spiritual cosmology and outlook as well as things like race-based and gender-based privilege, and life experiences such as harassment and assault, or even where we live, what we look like, and what our bodies can do.

To use myself as an example, I am oriented towards seeing gender-based violence, having lived in a body often read and understood as femme or feminine. I am always hyper-aware of microaggressions, sexism, and misogyny; I know what hatred of women, femme, and gender fluid/creative people looks like in both its explicit and implicit forms. I will always be oriented to be aware of these things; I am facing towards them.

It can be helpful to know about our orientedness – both the aspects of this we choose and have control over (such as our job, career, and training in school, religion of choice), and those we don't (sexuality, gender, race, heritage, culture of origin, disability). Orientedness helps us understand what we know we know, what we know we don't know, what we don't know we know, and what we don't know we don't know. When working with magic and diving into spirituality, it can be important to at least spend some time reflecting on all of this, so we can better understand why we're doing magic, for what means/ends, and what type of magic would best boost our efforts.

WHERE DO YOU WANT TO GO?

Once we have an idea of where we've been and where we are, we can begin to draw out the map of where we'd like to go.

If we don't take the time and energy to connect with any vision of our future and what our ideal circumstances might be, if there were absolutely no limits, we hold our magic – and ourselves – back.

Visioning the future can be scary. Many of us might not have even imagined we could live as long as we have – let alone have a range of possibilities wide open to us.

It's not uncool or cheesy to dream: to daydream or nightdream about who you want to be, what you want your life to be like. It's okay for these dreams to be big, lavish, flashy, simple, or what other people might call unrealistic.

Dream anyway, vision anyway, map out your ideal life anyway.

Cultivating an awareness of where we want to go is so important in spiritual work, but it is especially crucial when we work with magic. Magic isn't just about sustaining the present; though it absolutely can be – magic is all about possibility. Magic is a seed and all the power and potentiality within that seed; we begin with a seed first – at least one – before we can blossom into a tree or leafy vegetable or luscious flower, visited by happy bees, pollinating, chilling, flying around and being cute.

In order to get to where we're going, we first need to draw a map.

It can be scary to own what we want. It can be scary to pull out the parchment paper and draw out our next steps, paint the picture of who and what and where we feel bursting forth at the seams, who we feel is within us waiting to be born and reborn. But, to do magic is to pull out that parchment paper, and to design the life you wish to create.

To do magic is to move towards it.

To do magic is to be in a continual process of co-creation, of being in life as collaborative and artistic unfurling – in other words: the magic of manifestation. For our magic to work, we need to have a clear intention, and be able to communicate it clearly to our collaborators.

To do that, we need to know who we are, where we've been, and know where we want to go.

Connecting with Culture

Culture is a word that seems to encompass everything – what groups of humans do, think, and produce, with one another and alone. I struggle to think of anything that can't be included under the vast canopy of 'culture,' but the word is usually used to refer to spiritualities, religions, art, norms, behaviours, philosophies, cosmologies, thoughts, customs, laws, food, and more – ways of doing and being with one another, often in some kind of cohesive way. A broad sweeping discussion on what is and isn't culture is very much outside the scope of this book - though, trust me, I am incredibly tempted to write one anyway!

Why talk about culture and connecting with it in a book on witchcraft and magic? Well, because religion, spirituality, folklore, folk custom, belief, ritual, and many other things associated with these – mystical art, writing, music, dance, food and talismanic objects – are expressions of culture. Even if your own spiritual cosmologies come from your own mind, they likely have roots someplace; your spiritual ideas and your magical practice come from somewhere – even if it's the accelerationist social media landscape that most of us now find ourselves firmly within.

Over the years, I've seen practitioners lean into different approaches to culture. Some people seem to see authenticity only in what they perceive as other-to-them – the exoticized, romanticized, mysterious, far-away. One way this can manifest is when folks feeling a personal dearth of 'culture' seek to consume that which they see as rich-in-culture. I've observed this phenomenon most among white middle-class people in settler societies – who may feel distanced from or alienated from their own heritage. White American culture is so pervasive that white Americans often forget that it is, indeed, culture. (As an aside, many far leftist commentators seem to forget that whiteness isn't monolithic in a globalized context, and that a lot of cultures which are incredibly different and in conflict with each other are often horizontalized under that umbrella term.)

We see this romanticism in the seeking out of exoticized Eastern religions, be they Buddhism, Hinduism, or otherwise. On the other side of things, some practitioners move into their own heritage for inspiration and guidance into their own spiritual beliefs and practices. Growing up in both Canada and the United States, I couldn't help but feel disconnected from my English and French heritage. To compensate for my feelings of disconnection from the world around me, in my tweens I became particularly interested in all things English – architecture, folklore, mythology, witchcraft. I had already grown up with English customs, food, expressions, and ways of being. When I visited England at thirteen I had at that point never felt more at home, or more like I belonged. Everyone had some of the same facial characteristics I'd been mercilessly bullied for growing up in the states. It was amazing to walk past buildings that were more than one thousand years old, and to go inside them! This sense of history, lineage, heritage, and tradition isn't something that exists in the same way in North America, outside of Indigenous communities. I can understand why a lot of settlers living in settler countries feel called to reconnect to their roots, however near or distant those roots may be.

UNDERSTANDING WHO YOU ARE

This is the part that most books on magic leave out – the importance of starting with yourself! In magic, everything starts with you. Who you are, what you believe, what resonates with you, where you've been, what you've experienced, what you've overcome, and where you want to go moving forward. What you want your life to be like, who you want to become, what experiences you want to have.

Not everyone's magical practice or experience of magic will be the same – and how absolutely beautiful and wondrous and divine that is. All magical teachers will be teaching from their own perspective – their own positionality, their own orientedness, their own life experiences, cosmology, and worldview. I am no different! I remember what it was like to pick up so many witchcraft books when I was a kid, and really not see myself or my beliefs represented at all.

And that's a big part of my inspiration for writing this one.

I know that from my vantage point, I'll never be able to fully understand what it's like to be the magical, wondrous, divine being that is YOU – in all of your uniqueness and your individuality. Even if we share some of the same identity-based characteristics, there's no way I can ever fully understand your experience. Ultimately, we are all so deeply unknowable to each other – and I see that as something to celebrate. How wondrous is that!

I don't need to know your exact day-to-day experience to help guide you to shape a magical experience that will feel aligned with where you're at.

I believe you can be an animist and a witch.
Atheist and a witch.
Buddhist and a witch.
Christian and a witch.

I believe you can have a rigorous Buddhist spiritual and meditation practice for twenty years, honour your Christian relatives, heritage, and holy dead, resonate with animism, and practice this fun and deeply transformative, life-changing little thing I call witchcraft.

Though I honour Wicca and its founders and popularizers for their innovations and contributions to the history and present of magic and witchcraft, I also want to say loud and clear that we don't need to be Wiccans to practice successful, vibrant, and meaningful witchcraft.

Magic involves collaborating with nonhuman beings – instigating change in conjunction with the wills of these beings and friends with whom we are in intentional, meaningful relationship.

We're all going to approach this differently – collaborate with beings differently, connect with them differently. If you've picked up this book, chances are something about my approach resonates with you. I don't see the beings all around me and with whom I am always already in relationship with as just beings to exploit and 'use' – I see them as collaborators.

I see you, too, as a collaborator in this space.
How will you create magic?
How will your magical practice look?
What spiritual beings will you work with?

What spirits?
Will you work with ancestors? Deities? Deity?
Do you love cooking as a form of ritual?
Baths and tea and walking by the beach?
Or are you all about candles and smoke – is that how you prefer to relate to magic?
What does your body like? What does it not like? Where do you store stress, pain, apprehension?
Are you working through some shit? Do you feel foggy about your intuition? Are you really busy these days, with not much time for slowness and stillness? Or has your world ambled down to a snails pace, slow seaweed float in the lake?

While my pokes and prods and insistences on self-reflection may not be what brought you to this book and this practice of witchcraft – and while you may be feeling a bit uncomfortable and angry with me for my nudges at self-looking – truly, all successful witchcraft and magic begins here, with ourselves as an anchor. What feels right to you, in your bones and your soul? What resonates? What's the difference between something uncomfortable in a good way, in a growth way, and something severely not aligned with who you are and what you're about?

In this book I may make suggestions where you're like, Fuck that.

That's cool.

While there are many guardrails I'll talk about – safety bits and pieces that are mechanistic in nature, that I really would recommend you not ignore – there's also a lot of room for your own innovation, your own creativity, your own affirmation of your own freedom to relate spiritually with the world around you, the beings around you, and you yourself, on your own terms.

Just because no one has written about your exact intuitions on magic yet doesn't mean your personal experience is irrelevant or untrue. One of my greatest wishes is to see more innovation within magical communities and conversations – with more people willing to publicly pave the paths they've been walking, to say, Hey, this is how I do things, even though no other book says it. More diversity of practice, more creative and innovative sharing, and more leadership can only help the practice and community of magical practitioners flourish and bloom into even further expansion and innovation.

If you spend some /more intentional time with yourself, figuring out who you are when nobody else is looking, you'll have an easier time connecting both on an intellectual and theoretical level about what magic is and what it does and how it works, and on a personal, spiritual, intuitive level. You'll be removing some barriers to connecting with, and maybe even discovering in the first place, what resonates with you and what doesn't.

This may sound at first glance like an anything goes approach – it isn't. I've made myself quite loud and obnoxious online about how gatekeeping, rules, standards, rigour, thoroughness, vetting, vouching, and thoughtful, responsible leadership can make for safer communities, magical or otherwise, online or in person or anything in between.

Communities are stronger when we have a solid grounding in who we are and where we come from, literally and figuratively. What are our roots? What experiences were formative? What do we love? What do we think is awesome? What sucks and what are we really and truly not about? What are our boundaries – both as individuals, and in group practice?

When we have a strong sense of self – and self as one node in a larger network of interconnected beings, in community – it's easier not to be swayed and sucked into groups that are a slap in the face to our own personal idea of what it means to act with integrity.

I include this section because I don't want to be a guru. I also don't want you to be taken in by one.

I don't want you to look at what I'm saying and use it as an excuse to abandon yourself, to get further away from your intuition and your heart and soul and your personal power.

My vision is for you to work with this book to get to know yourself better, to be more confident in what you believe and who you are, to feel more connected to your agency as a person in this world and as a witch, if you choose to use that name for yourself.

I want this book to help you become your own teacher, your own leader, your own authority.

Not in an arrogant, I-know-everything-there-is-to-know way, but in a way that you trust your own body and mind, trust your own spiritual experiences, and know that you have all of the power and ability and vision and resonance within you to create everything that you could ever want for yourself, magically, spiritually, or otherwise.

If you have given anyone power over you, I would love for you to take that back for yourself – to affirm your own agency, your own ability to transform, to create, to take up space, to manifest, to do magic, to be whoever and whatever you are, in your own full uniqueness and brilliance.

I did not write this book to create a bunch of Sabrina clones, or to say that my way is the one and only way for everyone. I've learned a lot over more than twenty years of practice, so what I have to say is based on keeping my hands in the dirt, overcoming lots of road blocks, and going on wild adventures. I've learned what resonates with me spiritually. I've learned how I want my magic to look. I've learned what feels right to me. I've learned the shape of my own integrity. I've learned to move away from other vibrations, to say no, to fall away.

So what I would like to do here is to create a container of sorts, in guiding you deeper towards yourself, more closely within yourself, even if you've traversed these dark paths and already have a good idea of the topography of your insides.

APPRECIATION AND APPROPRIATION

Increasingly, there have been conversations about appropriation in witchy and spiritual communities. And unfortunately, 'appropriation' sometimes feels as though it's expanded so much as to be a nearly meaningless word. In my experience teaching workshops all over North America and a few places in Europe, this seems to be quite a widespread issue. I can't speak to a fully global and international context, obviously – and it's common for folks in North America to feel that our context is the only context. North Americans also tend to assume our experience(s) with race and gender are global and universal, further muddying the waters, doing what seems to me yet another form of attempted domination, where we impose our activistic frameworks, experiences, and rage on contexts and countries where they don't apply or even make sense, exposing our own ignorance.

The polarized perspectives on this topic go something like this: One side thinks anything should go, since we are all human, and cultures and people are always mixing for reasons of both power and pleasure, and isn't it just racist and exclusionary to act or enforce otherwise? The other side often argues that no one from outside a cultural group or race should ever do a particular practice from that culture, period, especially if that culture is marginalized and/or has survived through hundreds of years of oppression from those with more institutional and systemic agency and power.

Who's right?

Well, I think it's all a little more complex than can be shared in pithy online infographics, which are overly simplified into extremes, often by first year undergraduates. People from the same cultures and communities can have wildly different thoughts on the line between appropriation and appreciation; any group of people, of course, can't be a monolith – they're always plural.

To use one example in the realm of magic, I've heard from some folks in Haitian Vodou that their practices are closed, and that outsiders are absolutely not welcome. Some folks in African Diasporic Traditions definitely feel as though anyone who isn't black doesn't have any place practicing for any reason, no matter how called or spiritually aligned they may feel.

On the other hand, I've chatted about this in depth with someone I was quite close with for some time, who was from Trinidad. He told me stories of his grandmother practicing what she referred to as Vodou, and said – without my asking – that if she were still alive she'd happily teach me if I wanted to learn. From his perspective as someone who grew up with this work, their practices were open and gladly shared, as long as people interested were sincere, they were felt to belong.

Attitudes around spirituality, religion, ritual, culture, race, and imperialism differ widely often even within the same communities – and of course, as this person reminded me, Haiti and Trinidad are two countries with very different histories and different cultural and racial makeups, especially in regard to imperialism and colonial rule. It's important to keep these complexities in mind, and to walk softly and curiously. This is far from my area of expertise, but I wanted to include this anecdote to share how different viewpoints can be within a community – in this case, the topic of African Diasporic religious practice in a black and Caribbean context.

Online, there is currently an unfortunate culture of outrage, where social capital seems to be heavily correlated to who can facilitate the most successful and frequent public shamings. I've seen groups of people cosplay as ethnic groups and cultures they aren't actually in, and mob harass and extort people. These efforts work because so many people are afraid to use their brains and question what is really going on and why, and whether people are who they claim to be. Remember, mob rule isn't automatically correct. Ask questions, slow down, and don't be so fearful and open minded that your brain slides out of your ears.

A lot of the discourse right now around cultural appropriation has a misplaced obsession with a pure, unadulterated origin - a desire to preserve a 'pure' moment in time that may never have existed, what philosopher Bruno Latour would call a 'freeze frame.' This movement towards an exaltation of the 'pure' reminds me in some ways of right wing fundamentalism, which is also obsessed with origins and purity. To move towards purity is a distinctly modern behaviour, as Latour tells us in his book *We Have Never Been Modern*. To focus excessively on unadulterated origin is to freeze frame - to see something as static, which it can never be, nor ever was. In *On the Modern Cult of the Factish Gods*, Latour writes, 'thou shall not freeze frame,' and I agree. Nothing is ever pure, we are always already adulterated, mixed, in flux and in flow, always changing. To suggest otherwise is to ignore history, and reality. In many protectionist rants about cultural appropriation what I often see is a desperate desire to control - to control a narrative, but it is sometimes also an attempt to make up for what may be felt to be lost time, perhaps these social justice warriors weree not as immersed in what they see as 'their' culture as they wished they had been growing up. I can understand that sense of loss and the desire to mourn, but a protectionist, purity-driven attitude is ultimately a fundamendalist, totalist belief system.

The perpetual outrage and conflict culture of the internet seems to oversimplify everything into black or white, this or that, right or wrong, good or evil, oppressed or oppressor, woke or violent. Silence is violence, apparently, but so is speaking up. My view used to be a lot more simplistic than it is now, and I am grateful for the many conversations I've had with people in my life and with the books I've read for deepening my understanding, away from the purity politic of the often totalist 'justice'-oriented left. There's a lot of shades of gray in between the black and white, and things are always way more complicated and interesting than most Instagram infographics would lead you to believe.

Communities are not monoliths; there will always be disagreement from within the umbrella of a particular practice or group of practices about whether or not outsiders are welcome, and if so, how, why, and under what circumstances. For some teachers, if you're sincere, genuine, patient, and not entitled in your seeking, they're happy to welcome you into the fold.

On a personal note, almost all of my magical practice comes from within my own cultural heritage – English, Scottish, French, Canadian, and American. That being said, I do work with one saint that is outside of that. I've been to her temples, have many of her rosaries, had amazing conversations with those who tend to her temples and lead services in devotion to her. I've kissed her feet, was moved to tears in her temple, happily listened to services honouring her in a language I don't fully understand. I spend as much time with her as I can. I have statues and iconography of her all over my living space. I have a tattoo of her and will likely get more. I am committed to learning her language one day. Of all the spiritual beings I work with, it is to her that I am the most devoted. Would I be open to being trained in practices outside of my ethnic heritage at some point? Absolutely. I find that generally the spirits don't care too much, as long as someone is genuine.

Many people don't know their heritage. There are so many reasons we might not know exactly what our roots are.

Does that mean those without this knowledge can't safely dive into spirituality and magic? Are people who don't know their ancestral heritage doomed forever to a state of spiritual paralysis?

Of course not. Not everyone has the privilege of access to loads of information about their heritage and ancestry.

Sometimes the spirits choose who they choose.

Sometimes, a spirit, goddess, saint, or being from outside your own heritage may feel called to connect with you and speak with you, may choose to help you in your magic. If this is the case, I would encourage you to learn as much as you can about the context from which that spirit or being was birthed, so you can engage with them as respectfully as possible, if you wish to engage. I know I was shocked when the saint I mentioned before wanted to work with me – I didn't know anything about her, had never heard of her, and now we've been working together for more than ten years. Why did she choose me? I have no idea, but we definitely vibe – and whenever I've visited her places of worship, I've been welcomed with kindness by all of her other devotees. I visit those places with reverence and respect, and walk softly.

When we're thinking about whether or not something is appropriation or appreciation, here are some things to consider.

Ask yourself:

- Am I interested in this spirituality or form of magic just because I find it 'exotic' and 'other' and therefore more magical, because it's from a culture new-to-me? Or am I genuinely interested because I find the ideas resonant with my soul in a deep, meaningful, and authentic way?
- Am I just looking for a way to add a splash of something interesting or different than what I'm used to to my personal brand? Would I still be as interested even if I could never post about it on social media?

- Do I feel entitled to get all the info and be invited to learn everything immediately, or am I happy to be patient, wait, and trust the process, even if it's slow and lifelong?
- Do I feel motivated to monetize this knowledge as soon as I get it?
- Am I willing to do a lot of research to understand more about the tradition?
- Am I willing to accept that there are some things I may never know and understand?

So, what exactly is and isn't cultural appropriation?

It's going to differ based on who you ask, though there are many commonly agreed upon things that definitely fit the bill.

Ever heard of smudging? Often times well-intentioned but ill-informed people will refer to them lighting a bundle of dried white sage and waving it around to cleanse a space with smoke as smudging. However, done outside of a particular context and cultural milieu, this actually doesn't look anything like a smudging ceremony led by Indigenous folks – it's just a smoke cleansing. Smoke cleansings can still be powerful and effective - they're just not smudging, which is a word that refers to something specific.

Unfortunately, everyone on the internet seems to feel they are an expert these days, and many groups are popping up online, founded by ill-informed but maybe well-intentioned teens, citing everything under the sun as cultural appropriation. Unfortunately, some folks are so invested in not causing offense, being above board, and doing good, that it seems like some of their critical thinking, vetting, research, and assessment skills have completely vanished, were they ever existent in the first place. I've seen people on the internet try to claim things as banal as eating sushi as cultural appropriation, and attack others for begging to differ.

Wanting to do the right thing and not wanting to cause harm, are not reasons to throw our vetting and research processes out the window. Talk to lots of people, read lots of books, do your research, consider the source(s), think hard, reflect. Unfortunately, with the rise of online mob culture, we have seen people sometimes claiming false identities in order to bully people into submission, in order to say something is cultural appropriation when... it isn't. I've also seen folks capitalize off of the guilt many white folks have in North America – and I've seen bullying linked to extortion. The internet is a wild place sometimes, and it's the primary source of information for many people.

Context is important, sources are important, conversations are important. It's taken me many years to learn to cultivate and listen to my own anchor in regard to this topic, rather than simply swaying with the whims of certain online circles, in a desire to conform to the current 'correct' thought of the day.

Think for yourself, ask questions, never stop learning, walk softly, and stay curious.

The Question of Eclecticism

When I teach magic and witchcraft, I encourage my students to touch in with themselves as a starting point. What do they believe? What's their background? Does it resonate? To what extent? If not, what does resonate?

Often an approach that starts with the seeker rather than some kind of external authority or standard gets referred to as 'eclectic' – that is, something that draws from multiple influences, awarenesses, philosophies, and inspirations.

One criticism that often gets lobbed at anyone with an 'eclectic' practice that comes from their heart and intuition – and which may be a result of some exploration of mixed cultural heritage, or even just genuine resonance with spiritual practices outside of their bloodline, is that if it's not from your exact heritage word-for-word exactly, then you're being culturally appropriative, or that eclecticism is just colonialism by another name. While I do believe that cultural appropriation is a problem, omeone genuinely resonating with a practice and/or religious framework that their family doesn't practice and doesn't come from their culture – and practicing it full-heartedly for years, with an awareness of all these complexities and more - doesn't sound appropriative to me.

Of course, we always benefit when we consider the diverse and intricate histories behind practices we resonate with, whether they come from 'our' own culture or not. Thinking about questions of power and influence, coloniality, survival(s of people, practices, rituals), is crucial. And at the same time, sometimes we just genuinely resonate with what we resonate with. While it is undoubtedly true that certain practices taken up in certain ways by folks outside of it will be seen as disrespectful, offensive, and superficial, we also need to be careful about and aware of the tendency to essentialize, and how that, too, can be harmful – to assume that just because a person looks a certain way or we interpret them as belonging to particular identity groups, that we can assume they have particular characteristics, values, religions, etc. This is objectification and dehumanization by another name. People are not symbols. None of us can be distilled neatly into a list of identities.

What is essentialism? Essentialism, in the colloquial turn of phrase, involves painting with a very broad brush, and making assumptions about all people of a particular group or identity. Sometimes, though not always, internet advocates rail against appropriation by relying on ideas of essentialism in order to back up their claims.

Another word for 'essentialism' – albeit overly simplistic – might be stereotypes, combined with ideas of purity and determinism.

We can't tell what people believe by looking at them; we can't judge it by knowing their race or gender. Maybe the nonbinary femme in your philosophy class – an outspoken feminist, always bringing up issues of gender-based violence against women, femme, and AFAB (assigned female at birth) people – is Catholic and absolutely loves going to church, or maybe they're Wiccan and only work with hyper-masculine male deities. Everyone's practice is deeply personal, and I find I feel best and have the most fruitful, meaningful experiences with others when I don't operate from a place of assumptions.

Sometimes people see eclectic practitioners – who may be drawing from multiple aspects of their identities and life experiences – and assume that there is no rigour or depth there, just because inspiration comes from multiple influences, many of which may be near and dear to that practitioner for so many different reasons. To be clear, I'm not advocating a careless, thoughtless, 'buffet-table,' approach, which simply rides trends and follows what's 'sexy' right now. It's possible to be spiritually interdisciplinary, and to have depth in that inter- and multi-disciplinarity.

You don't need to tell everyone everything about your heritage in order to practice what feels right to you. No one is entitled to know anything about your spirituality, your identity, your history. Share when you feel moved, when you feel comfortable and connected. There's a disturbing trend I've noticed online, where total strangers will choose someone to harass, that they don't know, have never met, and have no relation or connection to, and ask them incredibly rude and invasive questions – in order for that stranger to be judge and jury on the validity of that person's spiritual expression. You don't need to fall prey to this, or prove yourself or explain yourself to anyone. If someone is coming at you like that, they likely don't have any interest in building a meaningful relationship with you. This type of person doesn't care what answer you give – it won't be good enough.

Some of those questions may be unsettling – and it's okay to feel unsettled. Actually, I find it quite important to ask ourselves what we're doing, why, how – if it feels heart-led, soul-ful, authentic, and true. Getting uncomfortable isn't something to run from – it'll help you ground yourself confidently in the 'why' of your practice. Maybe you step away from some practices, move towards others. It's all part of the process.

But please, please, please: don't let the invasive identity police invade your consciousness. Stay true to you. It's okay if you keep a lot of your reasons, motivations, identity, family history, and resonances private.

Blood Family and Adopted Family

Not everyone knows their birth or blood-related family – either one parent, or both. There could be so many reasons for this; life is complex and messy and rarely straightforward. I actually feel like this ancestry stuff is more complicated for more people than it might at first seem.

Perhaps you don't know much about one or both of your birth parents – maybe one parent left the family, maybe you are a child who comes from an unwanted violent sexual act, and you'd rather not know much about that side of your genetics. Maybe your family worked with an anonymous sperm donor, and despite efforts, you can't access anything about your genetic heritage. Maybe you were adopted into a loving family; maybe your adopted family is of a different culture and heritage than that of your genetic parents. Maybe you do know your birth parents, but you aren't comfortable reaching out to them for any information about your heritage due to years of abuse. Maybe your family migrated fleeing a war or other terrible circumstances, and leaving papers, photographs, and cultural heirlooms – or even names – behind was a matter of survival. Life is often a whole entire mess, and this is particularly the case when it comes to family – both genetic, and adopted.

I'm not listing all this stuff because I think blood family or genetic family is always terrible – of course it isn't! That stuff can be a very grounding, rooting, loving anchor for many people – a sense of continuity, of lineage, of heritage, of culture, of family. I don't think family or connecting with heritage always sucks; to the contrary, I'd just like to make space for the experiences of those whose relationship to family – blood or otherwise – isn't talked about.

There are a lot of folks who don't have access to any information about their heritage, no matter how much they want it. Others know a little, but not much. Coming to terms with this stuff can be tough, whether it's accessible or hidden. Parts of our heritage may remind us of parts of our family we don't like, or even feelings around abandonment, frustration, sadness, mourning, or any number of complicated emotions. Others may identify more with their adopted family (or even chosen family) than anything – and that's also a completely valid path.

You don't have to dive into the heritage of your birth family – genetic, cultural, whatever. Ultimately, you don't really have to do anything other than what you want to do. You're not a bad witch, a fake witch, or not good enough, if you're not doing spiritual work to heal or uncover or connect with your ancestry, genetic or otherwise. This is a path that feels good to some people, and not to others. In the current discourse in witchy spaces, it may sometimes feel like if you're not speaking in your ancestral language and baking foods sacred to your heritage, that you're the odd one out. Again, accessing information about our heritage and ancestry is a privilege that not everyone has access to – or even wants to access. Maybe you can access it, but sure as hell don't resonate. Also completely valid.

Your spiritual path – and your anchors for connection – are for you. You don't have to spend all your time doing witchcraft to connect to ancestry and heal your lineage. I mean, you can! But it's not everyone's path, and there's no shame in that.

Some may wish to honour both birth heritage and ancestors, as well as ancestors of their adopted family. If this resonates with you, the more the merrier!

WALKING SOFTLY: RESPECT

Wherever you arrive through wading through these challenging ideas, there are two main points I'd like to get across: the importance of rigour, and the importance of respect. That, for me, is how all of this can be summed up.

Wherever your spiritual and magical practice takes you, I hope you can walk with respect: respect for yourself and your integrity, and respect for the integrity of other people.

I hope you respect yourself enough to love yourself, to have faith in yourself and your magic, to not abandon yourself or your journey when things get tough, or when you're questioned, by yourself or others.

This also means respecting yourself enough to know when to tell other people to fuck off, or when to block them and protect your peace. Not everyone is worth your energy and time. Stepping away from an uncomfortable conversation out of shame and embarrassment about all we need to learn is very different from stepping away from mob harassment, abuse, disrespect, slander, and coercion.

In the former situation, I'd recommend staying present, sitting with the discomfort, and committing to grow and learn in conversation and in relationship, and even alone in the process of internal reflection. In the latter situation, I'd recommend reminding yourself that there will always be some people with whom it is never possible to have a respectful and compassionate solutions-oriented, growth-directed, mutualistic conversation. Some people are committed to misunderstanding us no matter what, and aren't interested in repair, they're interested in power through victimhood.

I hope you respect the perspectives of others, and respect the practices and cultures you don't know much about. Respect the time it takes to learn, to research, to gain skills, to get good at something.

WALKING DEEPLY: RIGOUR

Walking deeply means not just skimming the surface. It means going to the library or bookstore, grabbing twenty books, and still not being done. It means continuing to practice over days, months, and years, putting in the time to understand and deepen into the practice you're compelled to explore and root down into. By rigour I don't just mean books, though that's definitely a part of it! Maybe research will make you see your spiritual practice differently, and maybe it won't. Either way is fine. But it's important to know our roots, at least a little bit, in the ways that we can.

Rigour also means seriousness, means commitment, means sincerity, vulnerability, and trying hard, without embarrassment or shame.

Rigour is not ironic, it is not too-cool, it is not just trying to be funny. Rigour takes things seriously. Rigour acknowledges that things matter, that there is something at stake here, that there is something beautiful to be gained, that transformation is possible and it is desired and it is happening every day all the time.

Cultivating a Spiritual Team

Chapter Four

CONNECTING WITH SPIRITUAL BEINGS

When practicing magic, one crucial element to build and have in place is a spirit team. This often starts out with just our ancestor spirits, anyone who was or is close to us who has passed. Sometimes these are folks whose names we know, sometimes it's folks whose names we don't know. Either way, and even if you never get any exact names, I feel it's crucial to try and make this contact. If you're not ready for it right now, that's okay! There's no rush; you can shelve it and return some time in the future if it feels aligned.

If you don't have any interest in working with human spirits, try connecting with the energies of plants, or of place generally or specifically. If you prefer to use language like 'God,' 'the universe,' 'infinite intelligence,' or even 'Spirit.' Figure out what your cosmology is, what you believe in, and what phrasing and framing feels good and true in your soul. Are you monotheistic? Polytheistic? Do you even care about divinity – or are you more into spirits? Do you feel moved to connect with energies of the land?

The ideas behind what I'm writing here all come from my particular positionality—a person who grew up and still lives in North America, who grew up in Spiritualism, and who practices an intuitive, mediumistic form of contemporary witchcraft deeply influenced by many forms of Western occultism.

That being said, I've done my best to make the suggestions in this book applicable to everyone, regardless of your religion or spiritual beliefs. Christians can practice witchcraft. So can atheists. So can Buddhists. Magic and energy work are simply series of techniques and practices that are compatible with pretty much any belief system, whether it incorporates divinity or spirits or not. Maybe it feels better to you to connect with gods and goddesses than it does spirits. Or, to different aspects of yourself and your mind – archetypes and symbolism, influenced by varied branches of psychology.

When you connect with spirits, and build close, trusting, meaningful relationships with them, they can help you transform yourself, transform your relationship with where you live, with who you are and have been, and where you come from. They can help you have healthier energetic boundaries. In turn, we can honor them, give them our time and energy, pay them in friendship, offerings, tribute and homage in gratitude for their energy, teachings, and support

Types of Spirit Connections

There are so, so many types of spirit connections! From recently departed loved ones to distant ancestors, to helpful spirits who become helpers, friends, and guardians – there are spirits for everyone!

Jokes aside – I outline some different types of spirit connections here. Some may resonate with you, some won't – and hey, maybe absolutely none of it will. That's alright! My purpose isn't to give you a to-do list, but to create openings for exploration, resonance, curiosity, and connection.

Ancestor Practice

I feel most supported in my spiritual work when I expand my definition of what the word 'ancestor' might mean.

It hasn't always felt safe or desirable to me to connect with familial and blood ancestors, and it might not be for you, too. While connecting with our birth and/or familial lineages can sometimes be incredibly powerful, healing, and cohesive experiences, this definitely isn't always the case for everyone.

If you're not comfortable going there now, you might change your mind in the future – and vice versa! There's no one way to approach this. Follow your heart and your gut, and your intuition, to learn what feels most right for you in this moment.

You might be wondering what other kinds of ancestors there are, if I'm not only talking about family! I'll speak from my own experience as an example.

I feel connection and lineage with role models and past icons who share aspects of my identity, values, and life experience, and also inspire me in who I want to be and what I want to achieve – for me, the most important labels and affinities here are around queerness, gender, artists, and occultists. Though I'm not related by blood or genetic heritage to those I choose to honour, we share cultures of queerness, of art, of femme, of spirituality. I love to connect with them, pay homage to them, and when I can, visit their tombstones and leave offerings. If you find you're not too interested in family of origin work at the moment, this can be a great way to spiritually explore concepts and experiences of lineage and ancestry, from within a different angle and framework.

BLOOD FAMILY ANCESTORS

We all come from somewhere. We all have blood, heritage, lineage. The people who birthed us had culture, lived in and were born in certain regions. Maybe they moved or migrated somewhere along the journey, maybe by force or by choice. Blood is such a complicated topic that I'm almost worried to bring it up here, lest I sound like a complete essentialist or purity politics person (which I am not).

Blood quantum has been critiqued by many Indigenous scholars and others. Does your genetic heritage really matter, if a community accepts and loves you as their own? This is such a personal question, and we'll all have our own way of relating to it, as will all community groups and heritage-based/cultural groups.

How far you want to go into researching your heritage – genetic or otherwise – is completely up to you. What meaning would you get out of knowing more information? What would its significance be to you?

I also don't want to erase those whose stories are much more complicated than my own: people who are adopted, including cross-cultural adoption, and anyone whose migration stories span many countries, folks whose records and knowledges of where they come from have been lost to legacies of slavery, fleeing war and genocide, and the violences of colonialism and imperialism. Information about who we are and where we come from is a lot easier to access for some of us than others, and I'm aware even bringing up this question as a topic of conversation and consideration may be distressing or triggering for some.

Your blood family and your family of origin may be the same. It might be completely different! Or, it might have changed over the course of your life. Each of these life experiences is completely valid, and if you'd like to spiritually honour and acknowledge any of these aspects of your life, experiences of family, origin, and heritage, it's certainly something you can make the time and space to connect with, however much or little you know about these aspects of yourself.

CHOSEN FAMILY ANCESTORS

The notion of 'chosen family' is becoming increasingly common. Though it's been criticized by many queer and trans scholars and writers as missing out on an opportunity to highlight the importance and power of friendship and community (why does something need to be called 'family' in order to describe meaningful and loving closeness?), it's still a commonly used phrase, so I'll use it here while acknowledging some of the controversies in its labeling. Sometimes, families reject us outright, or don't accept us or parts of who we are. This can – obviously – really fucking suck, and so many of us seek experiences of family, love, friendship, support, and care elsewhere. These chosen families also have spirits – whether the dearly departed, or simply the energies swirling around the group – that you can call upon, honour, and invite into your rites, if you wish. Do you have a really close group of friends, or even a few cherished besties that feel like family? Have any of them passed on? If so, they belong in this group.

COMMUNITY ANCESTORS

Community can be another form of chosen family – or, if you'd rather keep some distance from allusions to 'family,' community can be its own kind of beautiful. People come into communities for so many reasons, but generally do so over some kind of kinship of similarity and shared concern, whether it be shared interests, values, spirituality, workplace, vocation, hobby, identity, or neighbourhood.

If you're a parent, you might have found some kinship and community through getting to know other parents in your neighbourhood; if you're a sexual assault survivor maybe you've found solace in getting to know fellow survivors in your region. Maybe you're a painter, and you feel most held and supported in your shared painting studio with a bunch of other artists. Maybe you're queer and trans, and don't know what you'd do without your trans siblings. Shared spirituality and religion is another place where many people seek community, togetherness, and solace.

Whatever community has looked like for you, it's possible to honour these forms of belonging and kinship in your spiritual practice, too – whether it's to honour a loved one in community who has passed, or to honour folks who have made moves in your community, who you look up to and look to for guidance. If you're a painter who has always loved the work of Jean-Michel Basquiat, you could honour him as a community ancestor. As a lifelong painter myself, I've always found his work to be deeply influential to me over my development and growth as an artist, and have honoured him by placing offerings at his grave whenever I visit New York. Similarly, maybe you're trans and look up to iconic trans ancestor Marsha P Johnson, and you'd like to honour her memory and spirit as a part of your regular spiritual and magical practice.

When we connect to community ancestors, we connect to a different kind of lineage – and for some of us, these bonds may be much more significant, meaningful, and supportive than those we are tied to by blood. It can be deeply freeing to expand our notions of lineage to include not just genetic ties, but other forms of family, community, and kinship.

Inviting these individuals into our spiritual and magical practice – whether that is simply to honour and acknowledge them, or to ask them for advice, can be a beautiful way to connect more deeply to ourselves, our history, and those who came before us.

THe HOLY AND HeLPFUL DeAD

You may also meet – either intentionally, or by happenstance – spirits who are not in any way related to you, but who, for whatever reason, feel compelled to hang out with you for a while. These spirits may be recently roaming, or around for quite some time. I call these beings the holy and helpful dead. They're somebody's ancestors, of course, maybe just not yours! And that's completely fine.

It may feel a little strange at first to open to the idea of working with the deceased who are not from your family – and a little spiritual stranger danger is never a bad thing. I've worked with some of these spirits over the years, with varying degrees of seriousness. Just because they're not related to you, doesn't mean they're dangerous. These spirits may teach you so much, and end up as some of your strongest allies, because they feel another kind of kinship to you.

MALIGNANT SPIRITS

Just like there are nasty, dysfunctional human beings that you may encounter in your day-to-day life, there are also nasty, dysfunctional spirits. When someone dies and their spirit continues to hang out, it doesn't mean their personality takes a radical, drastic shift, and they instantly become enlightened. Nope! People who are rude and want the worst for you when they know you in life, will generally feel the same way once they pass, and as you wouldn't take their advice in life, it won't be worthwhile to take their advice in spirit.

A lot of people seem to operate under the assumption that all spirits are kind, generous, helpful – or, to the opposite end of the spectrum, that all spirits are horrifying and malicious. In my experience, the truth lies somewhere in the middle. There are some nasty spirits, and some really helpful, kind, and generous spirits who really do just want the best for you.

Remember the energy work practices discussed in Chapter Two? Well, a big part of why I feel it's important to begin with energy work is that it really does set the stage for everything else to come – and it provides a lot of tools to help you take care of yourself when you do encounter a spirit or entity who really doesn't have good intentions towards you.

If you're worried about malignant spirits, try working on your energetic shielding and protective practices, and focus on establishing and maintaining strong boundaries. What rules do spirits need to abide by in order to maintain connection with you? To enter into your space, your sphere?

If you feel like you've encountered a malignant spirit who wishes you ill, you can be firm in your boundaries and request they leave. If they don't, revisit practices around banishing and cleansing. Just as in mundane life, it's okay to be sassy and fierce if they're not listening to any polite asks to leave. Your body, your mind, your space, your peace – these are all worth protecting, and fiercely.

SAINTS, ANGELS, AND MORE

It may surprise you to learn that I don't consider myself to be Christian, and yet I work with saints!

I love going to Christian churches whenever I travel around the world, and I have three different types of holy water in my fridge. I didn't grow up Christian, and so I find many things Christians take for granted, and common Christian narratives to be very confusing.

And yet I have rosaries.

And yet I work with saints.

I like to say that the saints I work with chose me, I sure as hell did not choose them; and if you told my ten-year-old-newly-magic-practicing self that my practice would evolve into working with saints, I would have wondered what exactly it was you were smoking, and why.

That being said, I do know that there are some ancestors in my lineage who were various shades of Christian – and so working with saints is one way to connect with and honour that part of my heritage, even if Christianity as a whole doesn't resonate with me. And this understanding – of the 'why' of my spiritual connection – only came later. Sometimes the understanding of a practice and why it resonates comes before we engage, and sometimes it emerges after. My suggestion would be to remain open to both.

So, if you're not someone who is a devotee of a religion that does emphasize saints and angels, you never know – these beings may still call out to work with you. If you're someone whose cosmology does involve an acknowledgment of saints and angels, you may feel called to fully focus on these beings as the foundation of your spirit team.

Sometimes, a saint will reach out and choose you. You'll see them everywhere – their name, their symbols, their imagery, pictures of them. Maybe it'll be the saint associated with your birthday, or your place of birth, or somewhere you've lived.

Or, maybe you go searching. Research stories of saints, holy figures, or angels – whose stories and attributes resonate with you? What energies or healing would you like to call into your life? When you sit with your research of each being, do any really jump off the page and feel fully resonant in your body and spirit? If not, are there any that you just can't get off your mind? Connecting with them may be a great place to start.

Personally, I have statues, saint candles, icon bracelets, and rosaries for the saints I work with. I love to give them offerings, call them into work ritual with me, and I love to wear jewelry devoted to them as I go about my day. Some of these ways of honouring saints may feel resonant to you, some may not! If you're not into rosaries, you can always create your own piece of jewelry, or buy something that reminds you of the quality of the saint you wish to connect with. I'd also recommend paying attention to their traditional feast day, and doing something to honour them during that time.

Saints aside, you may wish to work with and honour other holy or sacred figures – such as Mary, Jesus, Moses, or anyone else in any of the many spiritual books out there. It might resonate with you to connect with these figures, not as 'gods' per se, but as what I like to colloquially call 'fancy spirits' – more powerful and wise than your average dead person. Explore your interests, find what resonates – who you'd like to honour, and what form(s) of spiritual connection and honouring resonate most with you.

DIVINITIES

Within witchcraft and magic circles, there's a lot of pressure to decide which divinities we work with. These commonly take the form of gods and goddesses – and, even more frequently, pressure to select one 'patron' goddess and one 'patron' god. For those of us who have a more creative and/or fluid experience of and approach to gender, this may feel strange – I know it did for me, as a weirdo genderfluid nonbinary ten year old reading as many books on witchcraft as I could find.

While I completely respect people for whom a dichotomy of god and goddess, of masculine and feminine, is the most resonant – and hey, maybe this is you! – it's not the only divine formula out there.

Regardless of your gender identity or sexual orientation, you're free to work with whatever genders of beings you wish! Multiple goddesses, multiple gods, no goddesses, no gods; you can even focus on divinities that occupy more of a third space in terms of sex, gender, energy, and presentation.

When I was ten years old, I occupied a more strictly masculine form of gender presentation. I couldn't for the life of me resonate with goddesses or even 'womanhood,' no matter how hard I tried. Eventually, I just accepted that 'goddess work' wasn't for me at that point, and embraced my work with twin male gods. I honoured these beings for many years, and eventually my practice, its emphasis, and who my spiritual collaborators were has changed. Now, my main two spiritual collaborators are saints coded as female; interestingly, over the years I've become lots more feminine and today identify as female (long story for another time). Your collaborators may change as you change, and this isn't a personal failure. Our relationships with the people in our lives change as we change, too – the spiritual realm is no exception to this rule.

Something else I want to make sure I cover in this section is different ways to approach divinity. Some witchy folks resonate with hard polytheism, which is the idea that every being is separate and distinct – all goddesses are very different beings, despite their similar properties and attributes. Others will be soft polythesists – who tend to feel that – to keep with our previous example – all love goddesses are kinda just forms of the same thing. Other folks may feel like all this talk of gods and goddesses is only symbolic, or archetypal, rather than literal, and may operate under the understanding that honouring the divine is simply a form of us revealing ourselves to ourselves, of honouring and calling forth different aspects of who we've been and who we want to be.

Others still may feel that, while all of these pantheons of gods and goddesses and differently gendered divinities can be very fun and interesting, ultimately they are all faces of one big great spirit or god, separated into distinct parts so that our limited human consciousness can more fully understand this universal energy.

And, for some folks, divinity is singular, not plural – they may believe in one God, or one Holy Spirit, or just Spirit, or Creator, or The Infinite Universe. Maybe this is you! No matter what your take on divinity – singular or plural, hard or soft, literal or symbolic – you can incorporate your beliefs and cosmology into your practice of witchcraft and magic.

ASSEMBLING YOUR TEAM

Who are you drawn to? Who are you the most comfortable connecting with? Maybe you'd like to connect with your ancestors from another time or place. Maybe you know your long deceased family is from a particular country or continent, but you don't know much more than that. Maybe you know nothing. That's ok, and it definitely doesn't stop you from doing this work. You don't need to know any names or have any family photos in order for long-dead spirits to claim you as theirs. If you're adopted, you can still do this work. If you're estranged from your blood family for any reason, including neglect and abuse, you can still do this work. If you are open to it, and want to connect, working with your ancestral spirits is an option available to you. If you'd rather not go there yet or at all, that's ok too. Begin wherever feels good and aligned. Maybe working with animal or plant spirits feels most safe and protective to you right now. Lean into it.

A big thing here is to make sure we attract and welcome in the spirits that are well suited for us. Sometimes, our familial spirits will have left behind simple human nastiness or pettiness. When you set yourself up for this work, create the strong, fierce intention that only those spirits who are for your best benefit and who wish you well come through to connect. You want to make sure these spirits you build connections and meaningful relationships with truly do wish the best for you and want to usher you forth through personal transformation and protection. You may not like what they have to say, but if you align with spirits and entities who have already worked to heal themselves, and who have your best interests at heart, much of what they share with you will likely be for your best good. Always use your common sense. Listen to your gut and to your body. If a spirit suggests anything dangerous or something that sets off alarm bells for you, this is a spirit you should send packing. They may not be malicious or nasty, but you may not be compatible. And that's okay. We all have different boundaries and levels of comfort around various activities, and it's the same when connecting with the spirit world.

You may wish to work with divinities, or you may wish to work with saints, angels, or other spiritual beings, like animals or plants. When I was doing a significant amount of mediumship and trance work with animal spirits, one particular animal came to me as a guide. It was quite a surprising animal – not one often romanticized or thought of as cute or fierce. At first I was like, pardon? I had expected a cat, or something else I was familiar with and connected to, rather than an animal I had never given a second glance, and, to be frank, thought was kind of ugly. Our spirits can come from a variety of places and in many forms, if we're open to listen and make space for their presence and messages to come through. That surprising animal has become a much beloved ally and spiritual companion over thr last fifteen years. Be open to being surprised.

Chapter Five

Objects, Places, and Magic

Objects, places, and Magic

objects, places, and Magic

Objects, Places, and Magic

Objects, places, and Magic

objects, places, and Magic

Objects, Places, and Magic

Objects, places, and Magic

objects, places, and Magic

ALTAR PRACTICE

I always recommend setting up a little altar space for the spirits you'd like to connect with. If you hear that word and bristle, hear me out – an altar doesn't have to be fancy or ornate. You can make it uniquely to suit you, your comfort, and your needs. A regular altar-based practice can contribute significantly to maintaining meaningful and ongoing respectful and mutually beneficial relationships with members of our spirit team. You want to build a regular point of contact with your spirit(s) – like the go-to hang-out spot you have with your friends or family. One way I explain it is it's similar to checking in on your friends every now and then to see how they're doing, maintaining a sense of closeness across distance and time, an occasional hello just because.

So what exactly is an altar? Its form can vary widely, and is largely dependent on the flavor of your belief systems. For instance, on my altar I have multiple statues of both of the saints I do most of my spiritual work with. Have pictures or objects from your ancestors? Cool! Gather 'em on your altar table or shelf, if you're planning to work with them or honor them in any way. You can also have a few separate altars, if that feels better, like one specifically for ancestors, another for saints, and another for practical magical workings. Feel it out and see what resonates with you. I recommend regularly lighting candles and incense for any entities you work with, and giving offerings of fresh water or alcohol, or even coffee or juice, depending on what the spirits enjoy and if you want to cool down their energy or heat them up. I always have fresh flowers as an offering, as well as cold water, and sometimes other drinks or food such as fruit, candy, or even full meals for special occasions. Not sure what they'd like? Ask! It may take some listening to hear it, but eventually you'll get a sense of what's aligned and what's not.

Depending on your living situation, your altar's form may shift. Maybe you live in a one room bachelor apartment and don't want any visitors to talk to you about your altar. Maybe you live with family who aren't accepting of your path. There are more and less obvious ways to engage in altar work. Since I live alone, I'm able to have a large section of my living space dedicated to my spiritual work. You may not be able to do this, and that doesn't mean that your practice is less valid. Work with what you have.

You may wish to have all of your altar items in a box or trunk which opens and closes, so you're able to open it and set it up the way you like when you have the privacy to do so, and then pack it back up again when the time comes. You can also use a drawer as an altar space, if you really need to be covert about it, and sit with it open for a few hours before bed, or when everyone's out of the house. Or, you can even just leave your offerings in the drawer, and keep it closed—this way, at least you know your cats won't knock them over! Where there's a will, there's a way.

The point to all this is facilitating regular connection in a way that resonates with you, not teaching you how to make an altar that looks exactly like mine. If you make an altar exactly like mine, it probably won't work the way you want it to, since mine is based on my connection with my own practice, myself, and my spirits! Since you're a different person with different energy, different lineages, different visions, and different ways of doing and making magic, yours should look different.

You may come across some more Wicca-inflected books that will order you to set up things directionally—certain tools in the east, south, and so on. This has never resonated with me, at all, and I remember finding those instructions incredibly alienating as a young child reading about magic. Feel free to try out different types of altar arrangements and see what helps you connect more deeply and truly with spirit(s), with energy, and with yourself. What type of altar helps facilitate your connection? What do you need to feel connection and better notice energy around you? For me, what resonates is having a symmetrical altar created around the centerpiece of offerings (often flowers), with statuary of my saints at each side or visual representations of animal spirits I work with. Yours can look like this, too, or be super different.

WHAT IS AN ALTAR?

An altar can take many forms, but it often involves a broad flat surface, whether a shelf, table, or bureau of some sort; it's often elevated from the floor, though not always. It marks a space of spiritual doing, spiritual contemplation – devotion, faith, belief, and of course it is often a site of prayer, magical work, magic, and witchery.

My altars have taken so many different shapes over the years! One of my earliest altars was on a floating shelf that was in my closet – the lowest one. I'd sit on the floor beneath it, while I prayed, wrote in my magical journal, and prepared various objects for spell work and ritual. Now, I have a few much larger spaces out in the open – lots of surface room both to put devotional objects and offerings, and to get my hands dirty doing spiritual work.

ALTAR PRACTICE AS RITUAL

Altar practice is almost always ritualized – it's something we do and then return to, again and again – we attend to the altar again and again, rearranging our statuary, refreshing water and other offerings, replacing candles and incense when they're out. Maybe we switch up our altar for each full moon, for the solstices and equinoxes, for other holidays. These movements can help us cultivate an attention to time, to shift, to how we felt this time last year, last month, last week.

Altar maintenance like refreshing items which are in a way 'perishable' and require replenishing, (including offerings), can connect us to cycles and rhythms of both our environment, the culture(s) in which we find ourselves, as well as to ourselves.

WORKING ALTARS

A working altar is a space where you do magical work. This may look tons of different ways – it could be prayer, or grinding up herbs with a mortar and pestle. It could be carving your intentions into a beeswax candle, or painting your goals on a candle encased in a glass jar. Work can involve lighting candles, burning incense or herbs, working with water, creating various potions and concoctions, or even simply journaling by candlelight. This is all spiritual and magical work.

So, ideally, a working altar might have a broad flat space in which to actually do things in a comfortable way – where you don't knock anything over and can move about freely. You also might wish to pull up a chair, or have some kind of comfortable seating to accommodate you nearby, should you need it!

Small altar spaces can be a little cramped to accommodate a lot of process work – so I prefer to leave the smaller altars for honouring, as opposed to working – though at present, my working altars also honour the beings I work with.

ALTARS OF HONOURING

Another name for an altar of honouring is a shrine! You may be familiar with this word and concept; it often refers to a collection of imagery, statuary, or other material culture, with the intention to hour a particular spiritual being – often a saint or divinity, though it could also be the beauty and divinity of the earth, of the ocean, of the rivers near your home, of an animal spirit whose energy gives you strength. If this is your jam, consider gathering paintings, prints, and other imagery of whoever it is (and even things you know they like, or are typically associated with) – statues and other three-dimensional objects like jewelry can also be lovely.

However, you can also choose to do something quite radical, and create an altar to honour yourself. This could involve an honouring of your inner child, of your badass present day self, or of whatever version of yourself you'd like to dream into existence.

ALTARS OF MANIFESTING

A manifestation altar can look something like a full-on vision board, made kinda witchy! If you'd like to create a vision board with goal-oriented phrases of things you'd like to bring into your reality. If you'd like more money, you might want to take out a few larger bills and place them on a manifesting altar. If you're in the market to buy the perfect new home, you might want to cut photos out of magazines, or print out images of home listings that look perfect for you. If you're on the lookout for love, you might wish to load up on the cute red hearts, lovey imagery, and maybe even some chocolates, flowers, honey, and a sex toy. Or not! It's up to you. My general point here is that an altar of manifestation is a concentration of imagery, objects, and even words and journalings that, love notes to yourself and the universe, and anything else you can think of. Sometimes creating an altar of this sort can be a crucial step in opening ourselves to the magic of creation.

WHAT GOES ON AN ALTAR?

Anything you like can go on an altar! These can be spiritual tools such as wands, knives, incense, herbs; statuary or other visual representations of spiritual beings or lost loved ones; offerings like water, booze, snacks, or candies. Some folks prefer to keep their altars spotless and simple, and others (like me) like an ornate, at times cluttered and messy altar. It can feel like you - an extension of you and your energy, not like a chore or false facade you have to work to keep up.

An altar is a place where you honour yourself and your spirit team; it's also a space of magical work and action. Anything related to either of these goals can find a home on your altar! Or, you can keep these items hidden away, and only take 'em out when you're embarking into ritual territory. It's completely up to you.

You also don't need to go out and buy tons of things, either – simple items you likely already have at home can both represent and be spiritually significant.

OFFERINGS

What is the point of offerings? Do you really need to buy something that just sits there? Why prepare food and drinks for a dead person or a spirit or a saint or a goddess, or your higher or past self, if it's just going to go into the garbage or be left outside afterwards?

With magic, you often will get out oof it what you put in. And I'm not saying this in a bribery kind of way. It's not quite like that. But what we do know, is that our relationships—all our relationships—tend to improve when we put in sincere effort. Effort that is authentic, meaningful, and true.

Obviously, our effort won't always pay off—maybe we're in a shitty abusive relationship that isn't likely to get better no matter how many spells we do, or a dead-end friendship with someone who is too envious of us to maintain a real and meaningful bond. Sometimes it's best to leave with the awareness that we truly did our best.

In the successful relationships many of us do have, I think we notice that the more attentive and caring and appreciative and curious we are with our friends and loved ones—while respecting their individual autonomy—the more our relationships and connections with others thrive and bloom, as does our relationship with ourselves. This isn't about keeping score of who buys who dinner when and how much each meal costs, it's more about the sentiment, the intention behind the gifts, time, support, and care spent. Whether our best friend gets us the two dollar card from a discount shop, or a ten dollar fancy one, I'd wager it's the intent and meaning behind the gesture that matters most.

Give the best you can to the spiritual entities you petition, work with, and ask for help, when you can, as you can. If you're on a budget, work within it. If you have a little extra, share the wealth with your spirits, just because. Or, pick one day or event in a year to go big. This could be New Year's, or maybe your birthday or your saint's holy day. The specifics are less important than what it means to you. Maybe you resonate more with the full moon, or the new moon. If so, try checking in at least once a month, with the rise and fall of the moon's cycles, or as the month shifts from one into the next.

I always listen to the spirits' instructions on what needs to be done with the offerings I leave for them. On occasion, they go down the toilet or are dumped into the trash or compost bin. More often, however, I am asked to throw remaining water and liquids outside, or leave remaining food outdoors as an offering to the local creatures. If you do this, please also have an awareness of what animals and birds are in your local ecosystem and what they're used to eating. I live downtown in the middle of an enormous city, where raccoons, squirrels, and pigeons are used to eating pretty much everything and ravage the insides of trash bins. I will sometimes leave food offerings on a ledge on my roof, and sometimes I'll walk to a local park and leave it at the foot of whichever tree I'm called to. I've occasionally also left offerings in lakes or rivers, as per spirit instructions, and it's always been stuff I know wouldn't damage local fish or wildlife.

Some folks also like to leave offerings for their spirits at different locations that may be important to them, such as train tracks, crossroads, lakes, or rivers, instead of or in addition to being on an altar. Once you get to know your spirits over time, it may become easier to discern the places that are meaningful for them. If you're working with the deceased and you live near where they are buried, it might not be a bad idea to journey over to make offerings there every once in a while. With my personal practice, this has never been an option for me. Almost all of my offerings are initially done through my altar, and if that's the case for you too, it's ok!

MAINTAINING DIALOGUE

Altar work can be a great way to maintain dialogue with yourself, your goals, the universe, as well as your spirit team. Dialogue can be maintained through regular prayer, offerings, simple presence, and even the daily or weekly refresh of cold water or incense. Dialogue involves taking the time, space, and energy to engage in a ritual of connection and coming together – making room to listen, not only to speak. Magic rests on the shoulders of strong relationships, and over time, dialogue adds up to something deep, meaningful, strong, and sustained.

MAINTAINING RELATIONSHIPS

Relationality is, as we've discussed, a crucial component of magic.

If you think back to the earlier days of some of your most meaningful friendships, what comes up for you? Can you remember the awkward early hang outs, the tepid conversations – feeling unsure if you were at that stage of friendship yet where you could call them on the phone crying with an emergency?

But, over time – more drinks shared, more weekend adventures, more care packages left, heartfelt conversations had – acquaintances can become very good friends. One key ingredient here is time – friendships and relationships aren't built overnight, they take time to take root, grow, and mature. Maintaining and attending to a regular altar practice – whether it be of the working, honouring, or manifesting sorts – can help create an environment in which these spiritual habits lead to relational flourishing.

CONNECTING WITH NONHUMAN BEINGS

Objects abound in witchcraft! While it's possible to do magic with only yourself – your body, your mind, your soul, that's it – most folks don't practice this way, and prefer to work with various nonhuman beings: plants, animals, gemstones, water, metal, fabric, fire, wood, and more. Witchcraft today is often associated with consumerism, and not for no reason – walking into your average witchy, occult, or new age shop, you'll usually encounter a barrage of expensive objects slated to solve all your problems in the blink of an eye. While I'll never say no to adding a new object to my home, it's a little more complicated than much witchy discourse suggests.

My approach to object collaboration is animist in nature. Objects, like all else, have their own energies and essences, that we can vibe with in spiritual and magical communion. Even witchy books operating under the 'use' framework seem to imply that objects have power, have energy, that can be mobilized with intention, circulated towards our goals and desires. We collaborate with objects every day, without trying – this is simply a part of what it means to be a human in the world! However, when we work intentionally with objects in magic and witchcraft, we have the opportunity to put some of our animistic, spiritual, and energetic noticing into practice in new ways – which can transform ourselves and the world around us.

TOOL, BEING, OR BOTH?

In my cosmology, all 'spiritual tools' are also beings in their own right – with bodies, with experiences, with stories, with lineage, with vibrancy, with energy, with liveliness. Their bodies may look very different from mine, the folds of their consciousness may be ultimately unlike anything I am familiar with.

I don't put the human at the top of any hierarchy of being, and judge all others based on how 'human-like' they are – an animal does not exist any more than a plant does, just because the animal might be a mammal, and have arms, legs, and lungs, eyes, and a heart, just like humans do. Plants equally exist, even though what their sensations and experiences look and feel like are ultimately unknowable to us humans.

I extend this thinking to all beings, all bodies, all objects – those material forms many simply refer to as 'tools,' relegated to a space of 'that being exists to help me be.' And while that may be partly what goes on in magical collaboration, these 'tools' are regarded with curiosity, wonder, openness, love, and care – rather than thoughtlessly and feelingly discarded once its 'use' has been spent.

USING VS WORKING WITH

It's common in witchy spaces to phrase the working with nonhuman beings (objects, divinities, plants, spirits) as 'using.'

Though I'm sure my phrasing alternates a bit in this book, I prefer to operate under a framework in which nonhuman beings aren't 'used' – they're worked with, as collaborators, teammates, friends, family. 'Use' can imply an extractionist worldview – where anything outside the human exists not for its own sake, but solely for the purpose of helping us humans achieve whatever it is we have our sights on at the moment.

I don't feel that I 'use' candles or herbs, or even the saints – we work together as many actors, working together to achieve the same goal. I don't believe any other being exists solely to be 'used' by me. Indeed, I feel this worldview (a human exceptionalist one) has contributed to the widespread environmental destruction and climate catastrophe we find ourselves in.

When I intentionally step into a 'working with' framework, it reminds me to walk softly – to approach my nonhuman collaborators with love, care, and respect – for who they are, on their own terms, not only insofar as they're able to help me achieve my goals. We work together.

FEELING WHAT RESONATES

Not everything will resonate with you. That's okay! You may feel called to work mainly with water in your magic – or you may only do candle magic. You don't need to do any one particular type of magic – work with any particular type(s) of object(s) to be a witch. Witches don't all wear gothy clothes, lots of black, and only shop at medieval-renaissance-newage shops. You can still be yourself – with your own passions, interests, and tastes intact – and be a witch. No costume necessary, no mandatory purchase necessary

COLLABORATION AND CONSENT

In all collaborations and coming-togethers, consent is paramount. It may at first feel strange or unusual to take consent into consideration when we think of nonhuman beings, and especially objects – since they by definition don't have access to human modes of communication. A bowl or incense stick can't verbalize a yes or no.

That being said, you probably already have experience navigating consent with nonhumans, at least to some extent. For instance, one reason I love cats is their ability to very clearly communicate their boundaries; with a cat, it's quite rare to be unsure whether or not they're comfortable with you – if they're not, they communicate through body language, sound, and movement. They'll swat you or leave if they aren't happy.

While it may never be possible to fully know whether or not we receive consent from objects, I believe it never hurts to try, to walk with awareness, to make an honest and sincere attempt to connect with the energies of beings outside of yourself, to feel into the vibes. Have you ever stepped into a room and instantly felt a vibe – whether good or bad? Trying to sense energetic consent can work in a similar way.

For example, you might be a dandelion lover, like me! They grow absolutely everywhere in Toronto. Sometimes I like to go and collect some for bouquets around my home, to work with spiritually. When I go pick them, I hover my hand over them first – and feel the energy. Do I feel pushed away by the plant? Or do I feel a welcoming, 'Yes, I'd like to come home with you!' vibe? I've been close to picking plants before and have received a very visceral 'No.'

This may sound a little bizarre at first, if it's not something you're used to doing and asking of the nonhumans you work with in magic – but I'd encourage you to try it out, see how it feels, and see what you learn from being open to this form of dialogue.

OBLIGATION

Whenever we enter into any kind of relationship, we enter into some relationship with obligation.

This isn't an obligation to always be in relationship, but rather to always operate from a place of respect, honesty, and integrity – an obligation to, at least in my mind, be straightforward about your intentions for the relationship, what you can offer, how often you have the capacity to be present, where you'd like the relationship to go, and whatever else comes to mind.

Just as with any relationship with our fellow human beings, we can decide to step away from the spiritual relationships we build. But/and, relationships need to be cultivated in order to build and be successful, so try not to enter into any relationship you don't have the time to continue. It's not good manners to start off super excited, and then fall off without a word – it ain't nice to ghost a ghost!

Silliness aside, relationships do involve obligation. What's another word for obligation? Responsibility. Be prepared to check in with the spiritual beings with whom you're in relationship, to not just leave them hanging. If you start up a relationship by checking in and giving offerings, you don't necessarily have an obligation to have that same level of presence and availability every week, but you do have an obligation to openly and honestly check in with the beings with whom you're building relationship.

I'm not a huge fan of it when my friends ghost me – I understand that everyone has stuff going on, and sometimes it happens – but if it's a pattern, I might reconsider my friendship with someone who treats me like that, and if the behaviour continues… I might not continue to consider that person a friend. Similar can be said for working with spiritual beings. It's not about being tied to your spirit collaborators and seeing them as a ball and chain – it's about genuine, authentic cultivation of mutualistic and respectful relationships.

Successful magic with longevity – much like a happy, fulfilling life – is enriched by maintaining meaningful and strong relationships.

MAGICAL TOOLS: AN INVITATION TO AUDIT YOUR HOME

Tear apart all of your magical cupboards, to look around at all of your ritual supplies (herbs, oils, candles, tarot decks, statuary, bones, incense, charcoal, dried eggshells, etc) and reorganize. Separate it, see what you have, and make lists. What do you have too much of? What do you have not enough of? What do you need? What types of magical objects do you work with the most? What do you gravitate to? Do your stores mostly consist of herbs and candles, or are there like fifty tarot decks and a handful of tealights?

What type of magical work would you like to do? Take note of what your magical supply store needs. Having the right magical materials around at home can help you set yourself up for success magically. If getting started is a challenge for you, and you find yourself lacking in energy or motivation, it can be incredibly important to do what you can to keep your stores stocked up so you have a few things ready when you need them.

Sometimes, what we need to do – and the magic we need to do – in order to be aligned in our lives can't be planned. I always encourage my students to work with what they have, however skint their bank accounts or magic storage cabinets may be. There's no shame in not having that many supplies, and I guarantee that you have enough at home to work magic, no matter how bare your cupboards are.

While sometimes we may be able to luxuriate all day before a big ritual and do an enormous shop right beforehand, hitting up a few different candle and herb shops for just the perfect materials; we don't always have time to do this. Sometimes magic needs to be immediate, dynamic, responsive, and last minute, something we can do with literally no notice in order to protect ourselves or move our situation along in a way that best suits us.

I do plan many of my much bigger rituals, and go shopping beforehand, but just as often, my magic is impulsive and takes over me with absolutely no warning.

Impulsively, on the January new moon a few years ago, I rummaged around my existing candle storage, found something perfect that I had intended to use with a client, or even for myself much later down the line – a white marriage candle – and, after fixing it with rose and lavender, I got on my knees and prayed to my spirits. I prayed to know within one month if the person I was seeing was my match or not, and I asked to be shown many irrefutable signs. I asked the spirits to work in my best interest and show me the truth, even if it was painful. I kissed the feet of my saint statues. None of this was planned, it all came from my gut.

The candle worked fast, and I knew within days that the man I had been dating was not the right one for me, wasn't my forever person. This was not a magical moment I could have planned, or would have been able to plan. Love is a topic so close to my heart, it is my weak spot where I sometimes have trouble seeing my own life clearly. If I had taken a few more days to go to the shop to get a candle for this purpose, I would have completely lost my nerve, overwhelmed by fear of what I might be bringing upon myself. Having a few candles around for various purposes just in case enabled me to enact this deeply powerful working – even though when I bought that candle, I assumed I'd be using it for a client in the future, not for myself. Almost exactly one month later, just after the next new moon, I officially left for good, solid in my decision, difficult as it was. None of these important changes and transitions would have happened for me without that impulsive act of magic., and following my intuitive burst of feeeling.

Why am I telling you this story? Because if I hadn't taken the time to assess my magical cabinet a few months prior, I definitely wouldn't have thought to purchase the odd marriage or relationship candle. Taking a look at what I had, and reflecting on what my goals were for the next year at the same time, inspired me to buy a few things in advance in the off chance that a moment to use them revealed itself to me, whether for myself or someone else.

There's something incredibly special about harnessing the initial moment that something strikes you. There's a certain zest for life, a raw desperation, and visceral intention about that impulsive, chaotic feeling that can hit us at the most seemingly inopportune or random moments.

I usually organize my items based on what it is, rather than by magical purpose (for instance, there is no 'love' section in my cabinet, but there is definitely a candle section).

Personally, I have never ever thrown out magical tools. Ever. Objects hold massive significance for me, as trusted friends, allies, and and I like to think that my magical objects gain more potency the longer they are sharing space with me. They take on some of my energy, and become more personalized and powerful for use in my own work.

What can count as a 'magical tool' or collaborator? Literally anything you want! Though folks newer to this work might often assume that candles, incense, gemstones, and goddess statues are the only way to do 'real magic' – and this idea is often pushed at many new age witchy shops as well, unfortunately – in reality, you can do some powerful witchcraft with some toilet paper and dental floss.

Connecting with Place

It may seem obvious to say, but we are always somewhere. We are always in relationship with place, we are always in an environment, we are always situated, located, oriented, in ways that are shaped by the places we have been, and the place(s) we are. Place often becomes invisible to us as familiarity grows; when we travel, or walk down an unfamiliar street in a neighbourhood we've never been before (perhaps on a trip, perhaps on the way to meet a friend), 'place' is more visible when it's new-to-us.

Often, it can feel a little easier to intentionally connect with a place we've never been – which is why so many folks love travel! A twisting Parisian street, a sandy Cuban beach, a Tokyo shopping district (if you don't live either of those places!) can inspire a slowness, an attention to detail, a sense of curiosity, wonder, and deliberateness that we rarely access when in the place we're in all the time.

I'm curious about what might happen when we attune our attention(s) to building this sense of awe and wonder about the places we spend most of our time. Whether this is going on an intentional walk in your neighbourhood, learning more about the specificities of where you live (maybe colonial history, if relevant to where you are; maybe geographic history; maybe you'd like to learn about the plants and birds native to your neighbourhood and region). When we go on trips, some of us love to buy books about the cities and countries we visit – maybe we learn some of the language, learn how to cook the cuisine, learn important historical and cultural moments in that region. I find it super interesting that most folks don't do this about their own countries or cities!

However, I believe taking some more time to connect with place, with 'home' or even home(s), whatever and wherever that is for you, can only strengthen and boost our magic, can only help us to feel more connected to ourselves and the spirits of the earth, of the land, of the animals and plants, of the people who have walked before us. We can always listen more where we are.

COLONIALITY AND IMPERIALISM: SETTLER WITCHCRAFT

I was born in Montréal, Quebec, otherwise known as Tiohtià:ke – a region historically the gathering place of many First Nations and Indigenous people, the Kanien'kehá:ka Nation is recognized as the custodians of the lands and waters of Montréal. Now, I live in Toronto, otherwise known as Tkaronto – the traditional territory of the Mississaugas of the Credit, the Anishnabeg, the Chippewa, the Haudenosaunee and the Wendat. I've read some books about the histories of Indigenous peoples in Ontario specifically and Canada in general, and I intentionally seek out Indigenous film, poetry, creative writing, art, and sculpture. I haven't been to any academic conferences in a while, but when I did, I'd research where I was going – which Indigenous peoples' territories I would be presenting my research on.

Why is this important? I don't have any Indigenous-to-North-America ancestry. My mother's heritage is Quebecois – before that, French. My dad was born in England (and his parents before him, and even before). From what I'm aware, my heritage is pretty straightforward. This means my family came here from other countries – they were, in other words, settlers. Anyone non-Indigenous to North America, is a settler; including recent migrants like refugees.

All of the learning I've done has helped me to deepen my relationship both to this place where I live, and to myself, my ancestors, my past, and my present. I feel more connected to this land, knowing more about its history, and how families like my ancestors ended up here. I'm not too interested in moving to the United Kingdom or France (my French is terrible, and I find the UK too gloomy) – I feel at home in North America: spiritually, culturally, mentally, physically. I love this place, its vibes, its people, its philosophy and approach to life. I don't want to deny or erase my ancestry; I want to acknowledge it, honour it, and also honour the place where I am, where I will continue to be.

Why is this relevant to witchcraft?

Well, a lot of witchcraft and magic is land-based, or at least acknowledges the earth, plants, forests, rivers, and the natural environment. Witchcraft is, more often than not, associated with 'earth-based' spiritualities like contemporary Neopaganism, be it Wicca, Druidry, goddess worship, or animism. Many witchy books encourage folks to go out into the city park, into an urban ravine, into the country, onto the beach – to commune with a generalized 'nature,' a pristine, pure fallacy of romanticized 'environment.' This picture of the land is often divorced from material reality, both past and present – it can ignore histories of colonialism, empire, and capital; it can ignore present-day environmental catastrophe and decimation/pollution of environment. Isn't it perhaps important for people who claim to and desire to work spiritually with land and place to have some connection to history – both of the land on which they walk and do magic and pray, and also about the specificities of the circumstances that led them and their families to reside there? It seems important to me that folks working spiritually with the land, and with materials and beings that come from the earth, take some time to sit with this – particularly if you're coming from a settler perspective in one of the countries where this is especially relevant (I'm thinking Australia, New Zealand, Canada, and the United States, in particular).

If you're a settler, how does being a settler on these lands impact and shape your witchcraft and magic? I'm sure the answers will be different for everyone, but they're important (if sometimes uncomfortable) questions to ask. We don't have to linger there forever, but it's important to at least think about.

Of course, I'm writing from a North American context, with my head in the North American sand. There are so many global, international perspectives on this – power, capital, empire. Of course, North America isn't the only part of the world with a history of conflict between cultures and ethnic groups – it's typical for North American activists to forget that intercultural conflict happens all over the world, and always has. Wherever there's people, there's conflict and plays for power. I know there's a lot I am completely unaware of, and I'm sure the dominant narratives on some of the issues I've presented here will be very different outside of my own context. If you're in the UK or France or India or Ethiopia, you'll havve completely different context and awareneesses.

If all of this doesn't seem relevant to where you live in the world – okay! What stories of power, history, conflict, and conquest are relevant to wherever in the world you happen to be? If you don't already know all about it, how might you learn more?

It's never a bad idea to learn more about – and reflect on – where you live, and how different people have come and gone in that region, whether by choice, through conflict, through struggle, through joy. How has power (both positive and negative) circulated where you live, and/or where you're from? What conflict and power struggles have happened there? For me, in my context, this is an exercise in thinking about how being a settler on this land relates to, impacts, and informs my witchcraft.

For you, this might take a different shape, as you discover (or remember) how power and people have touched the lands where you are and have been. It doesn't mean you need to or should have any shame about where these questions lead you. I'm not a fan of self-flagellation and guilt politics that are rampant in far left spaces in North America and online. My point here is that more knowledge is never a bad thing. Do what you can to fill in your own gaps.

SPECIFICITY OF ~~THE~~ PLACE

Place is specific.
Place is unique.
Not all forests are the same, not all beaches are the same, not all lakes are the same, not all neighbourhoods in cities are the same.

One place is not interchangeable for another. It may be tempting to universalize all categories of place, and make generalizations about the country, the city, the suburbs, the desert, the beach, the jungle, the forest. Of course, some places may have overlapping vibes or characteristics, but every place, despite similarities with others, is completely unique, specific; exactly and entirely itself.

This knowledge fills me with wonder as I move about the world.

How absolutely exciting that each place I walk and move is unlike any other. This helps me stay connected to the marvelousness and specialness of all that is – and encourages me to listen as much as I can to the energies and beings that surround me, wherever I am. If you feel bored of where you are, I invite you to look a little longer, feel a little more deeply, ask more questions. Slow down and listen. Relax into where you are.

BEING HERE

It's common in some aspects of spiritual discourse to hear this romanticism of the elsewhere – rather than open into the magic of being right here, wherever that happens to be. Some folks preach the idea that we can really only do actual magic if we're in the middle of a forest, naked, dancing on twigs – surrounded by cool animals and birds. While that may be fun (and a quick way to get lots of bug bites), not all of us live in forests, or in areas where access to organic environment is easy to come by. And some of us hate 'nature' (due to allergies, dislike of mud and bugs, etc) and prefer to chill out in built environments.

Where you feel most vibrant, comfortable and connected to the world around you? Do you always need to depart from where you are in order to spiritually connect – or are you always able to cultivate an attention to vibes and leap into magic no matter where you are?

We don't need to go anywhere else in order to access magic, to access spiritual connection. There's magic, beauty, vibrancy, and wonder all around us – whether we're in rural farmland, or in a big city. Where you are is exactly enough. What might it feel like to commit to where you are – to see and feel magic in familiar contours and shapes?

PLACE AND MAGIC

Magic can come from anywhere – and magic partly always comes from place. Even if we do magic by ourselves, just by visualizing, no plants no incense no candles no nothing, our own human bodies are rooted in place; where we are and where we've been. We are always situated in (some)place – the histories of where we've been, the lineages of our families, the stories of where our relatives have been, our own stories about frequently trod loops of street or soil. We are always in place – we are never really no place. We're geographically somewhere: a city, a town, a suburb, a shack in a forest, a remote island.

Our home, too, is an important place in magic making. At the time of this writing, I've just recently moved into a new-to-me apartment on the other side of the city – very very different from my last tiny treehouse apartment in the middle of downtown. It was a haphazard, strange building with an uneven floor, and in the decade I lived there my landlord rarely repaired or checked anything. Regardless, my third floor one bedroom (with flat roof to suntan on, thank you very much) felt like mine, felt like home – we were two beings fused together. We felt each others' energy. That place always knew me so well, knew what I needed, knew how to hold me through trauma and pain and heartbreak – and also joy and success and creation. I bonded incredibly strongly with that space, though after a decade I knew it was time to go.

My new apartment feels strange still, and I'm learning its contours, its moods, its energy, where it wants me to place my art and my altars. It's a learning process, and we're slowly getting to know each other. Just like cities, neighbourhoods, or any outdoor environment, indoor environments and home spaces can also build a strong bond with us over time, and become co-creators in the making of magic. I did countless incredibly powerful life-changing rituals in my last space, and I know that the specificity of that place, and its own power, hugely boosted my magical efforts. And – it's because I built a relationship with those walls, over the course of a decade.

Each place has its own energy, its own personality, its own spirit. And it may show you a different face, a different vibe, than it may show to someone else. Just like we build relationships with other people, we also build relationship with place, whether built or organic, whether intentional or accidental. If you miss anywhere, long for anywhere – congratulations, you're in relationship, in connection, with that space and its energies.

Magic happens somewhere: in your body, in your apartment, in your town, your city. Place is a spiritual collaborator in all we witches do, like it or not: and so working intentionally to listen to place, to speak back, to relate, to express care, can only strengthen our magic.

CAN WE REST-IN-PLACE?
THE ETHICS OF RETREAT

Are you romanticizing the not-home? What stops you from retreating at-home, or at least in your city or neighbourhood? What might it mean to retreat in daily life?

In spiritual communities that are more earth-based, there is often talk of retreat, going into 'nature.' A lot of spiritual traditions suggest this, of course, but here I'm going to stick to what I know, which is contemporary iterations of Western magic; regardless of whatever shade of this you practice, it has been touched by lineages of Wicca and conversations that arose in accordance with it (and also, of course, reaction against it).

As readers of Ronald Hutton's *Triumph of the Moon* will know, contemporary Western witchy practice is linked to the development of a neopagan ethic, which is largely rooted in the bourgeois pushback to the rise of industrial production and the growth of cities in the 1800s. People with money and leisure time retreated out 'to nature,' to get away from 'it all.' This movement is based on conceptualizations of place that are dependent on purity: 'nature' as a pure space, pristine, untouched – which has direct ethical implications for those of us who live in settler societies, whose seizure of land has been and remains dependent on notions of land as empty.

This may seem like a lot of heavy shit to bring up; I mean, come on, aren't we just talkin' about going somewhere to take a break for a while? Who doesn't need a break! Why do we have to talk about imperialism? Come on! Enjoy things! Have a beer! Or, uh, some kombucha! Om! Namaste!

Okay, so let's rewind.

I do live in a big city, and I love it.

Toronto is the largest city in Canada and the fourth largest in North America. When I moved here from Colorado, it shocked me that seemingly everyone had a family cottage or home on one of the great lakes that they could go hang out at during the summer or on weekends. In the states, what I was used to was that only rich people had any second homes.

This took some adjusting, and to be honest, I still find the Canadian attitude that 'cottaging' is normative to be a little odd. One amazing thing about Toronto is that the city is pretty decently integrated with the natural environment – we have a waterfront, some beaches, an island, a ton of big parks. I know that this ain't enough for some folks, so we go elsewhere: to the cottage, on retreat, wherever, anywhere else but here.

What is retreat, anyway?

It may be useful to reflect on what this word means to you. Is it a departure or a break? If so, from what? To get away from what, to move towards what?

Where are you going, and what is your relationship to that place? Who will be taking care of you when you are there? Is this a place you feel committed to get to know and build relationship with, or is this a place you see and approach with a more extractive mindset – as simply a place to relax, a place without specificity that could really be a stand-in for any place that is not-home?

Are you romanticizing the not-home? What stops you from retreating at-home, or at least in your city or neighbourhood? What might it mean to retreat in daily life? Have you pre-emptively cut off home from the category of places in which it is possible to retreat? How might you rearrange your home/daily/etc situation to enable and encourage moments of daily retreat and connection?

I feel like when people say they want to go on retreat, what they really mean is that they want to feel connected, they want to feel less alone.

There is in some sense an irony then that we often retreat from the city into the country or the rural, often alone. But, what we usually move towards is connection not necessarily with other people but with the earth itself, with the land, with the planet and plants and breeze and water and twigs cracking under our feet as we walk, with the squirrels watching us as we travail a well-trod forest path. A connection to traditions of movement. Others trod this path before me, others will tread it again after I am gone. For many, it is somehow more easy to feel this way in a forest.

I get it. A lot of us have busy lives, full of work commitments and obligations to family and friends. We're overbooked, overtired, and often underpaid, with sleepy and sick bodies. So taking a break from this can be perceived as a way to refresh, replenish – and it often can be.

It may seem like I'm smack talking 'retreat.' I'm not!

I'm a Sagittarius, after all! I absolutely love to travel.

But while my passport has lots of fun stamps in it with many more to come, I am also a member of the stay home club. I'm all for movement and new experiences. I love it. But, and – it is so crucial to spend time in reflection, in examination of our impulse to move or lie still, to come or go. Sometimes the unhealthy, unquestioned impulse is to stay home, to be immobile, to steep in stagnation. But, and – sometimes, the unhealthy impulse is to retreat.

I invite you to consider (really and truly):

- Is the retreat far away or nearby? Why?
- What are your motivations for going on retreat and/or for retreating?
- What is the relationship between your retreat and the desire to escape? Is it merely escapism?
- Is the retreat a placeholder for making other changes in your life?
- Are you avoiding the importance of being able to connect to spirituality from exactly where you are?
- What do you hope to gain from the retreat?
- What do you hope to release, if anything?
- What is your relationship to the place you are going?
- Do you know much about the place you are going?
- Do you know much about the people there, if there are any?
- Do you know the history of the place?
- Will you continue to visit that place and build relationship to it?
- How will you give gratitude to the place for holding you, for making space for you, for sharing its lessons with you?
- How will you practice an attention to what is enough?
- How will you notice when you have reached the extent of your welcome, and/or what you can take?
- If you are collecting souvenirs or magical supplies such as water or plants, do you have offerings to give in return and in gratitude?
- How will you get to know the spirits of this place?
- How will you commit to treading carefully and with care on this new-to-you ground?

We don't belong everywhere all the time, and it's important to remember this. Can your process involve reflection and moving away from an entitlement to being wherever you want Can you walk softly on the spaces which do already hold you?

(Be)coming Home: More Ethics of Retreat

In the last section, we reflected a little bit about what it means to physically depart: to retreat more specifically (to a place) less broadly (philosophically, conceptually). Today, for the full moon, I'm thinking a lot about the search for authenticity and the perception of that search being predicated on movement. I'm thinking about access to leisure and how that access is influenced by access to capital, time off, and a non dis/abled body; access to an embodiment that allows us to feel safe and stable.

For me, I feel at home in the city partly because there are so many people around – volume feels like safety. And then there's access: to my apartment, friends, hospitals. It feels like a risk to be somewhere all by myself. To some that may feel like solace but to me it feels scary, like someone could find me and hurt me and that would be the end of that (or me). What happens if my body gives out (as it often does)?

What about the value in facing these fears, these feelings of unsafety, this risk and susceptibility – a very real sense of vulnerability acquired over time due to experience? What about the relationship between risk and growth – and is that really what we're searching for when we go 'on retreat'?

Retreat can be physical, or it can be internal.

There is always some interplay of both in all retreats, and often people will use a physical retreat as a means of instigating or accessing internal (be it mental, emotional, etc) change. Some retreats look more like shutting down, shutting off, going into oneself, being still and silent and alone – and that's it. These are the type of retreats we can do a bit more often because all it takes is time to ourselves, all it takes is our own body, our own choice to not speak or think or connect with others. Turning our phone on silent, putting it in the other room. Disconnecting the internet. For an hour, a day.

Retreat has an interesting relationship to mental processes as well, both voluntary and involuntary. Sometimes we may be thrust into retreat when we don't want to be, because that's how our brain is wired, for whatever reason. We may have some control over this, or we may not. This kind of distinction is crucial because it influences our relationship to concepts of retreat, as well as our relationship to our own sense of autonomy and movement, and how that relates to having access to things like actively choosing when and where to retreat.

For folks who do not have full control over when they mentally retreat, asserting agency over physical retreat (when that happens, in what circumstances, where, etc) can be ways to reclaim a sense of personal agency and efficacy.

I have CPTSD - and so sometimes I dissociate. I get very quiet and go into myself. This kneejerk reaction that my brain learned was a mechanism to ensure my safety during those tough times. However, now, even in the absence of abuse, my brain and body can react that way to stimuli that remind me of abusive moments. This dissociation is a form of retreat, a departure from the everyday.

No, it is not as enjoyable as a vacation to the Bahamas or a cute cabin in the woods after a year of being incredibly stressed out at work, but there is conceptual kinship here: the retreat occurs when a limit is reached or about to be reached. One is voluntary, one is not, one is fun and one is not; but both are responses to overload, a response to capacity being reached. Interestingly, an element of trauma therapy often involves exposure to the source of trauma, after a sense of safety has been built up.

Becoming strong and stable enough to withstand the trauma exposure often involves a retreat away from it, enough time to recover and regroup. The intentional retreat and re-exposure can lead to less dissociative moments in the long term.

An important aspect of this is that we do not live in a vacuum.

It's likely that our retreat(s) are impacting others around us, and impacting our relationships to them. It is true that we need to take care of ourselves: there's a reason why airlines always insist we put our own safety mask on before assisting those around us. Are there ways we can make these retreats – our absences – a more ethical and considerate process that acknowledges the social ecologies in which we are embedded? Giving folks a heads up may be crucial.

Let us for a moment return to the spiritual retreat. I see 'retreat' pop up a lot in conjunction with the new age, which seeps into contemporary witchy movements and communities, particularly those in North America. Many of our witchy shops also double as new age shops, an overlap that seems to me much less common in the United Kingdom and other parts of Europe. The new age, for some people, is all about getting good feelings. This is often achieved through the spending of money and the acquisition of objects and experiences; collection and conquest. These acquisitions are often related to what we perceive as other. Otherness is mobilized as a stand-in for the authentic, the real.

I feel as though this movement towards the elsewhere is all actually about a search for reality.

There is often a self-professed purity here, a paring down – to retreat can mean to discard the more obvious trappings of capitalist living: time at work, dealing with bills, partners, parents, kids, obligations, making money, waking up, feeling stressed out, trying not to have a meltdown, rinse, repeat, etc.

People retreat to 'get away from it all' and I think it is worth magnifying this 'it' – what exactly is being escaped?

What does it mean to connect with the authenticity inside ourselves, rather than search for it elsewhere? To acknowledge that we always already have the 'it' we wish to move towards inside of ourselves? Can searching elsewhere help us gain access to ourselves? What is this search for authenticity about, anyway, and why do we tend to assume it lives somewhere else, elusive?

When we retreat, what do we move toward, what are we moving away from? How does this relate to what is ingrained, and what is fresh? How does your retreating relate to cycles – both dysfunctional cycles and healthy cycles? Is going on retreat part of establishing a new cycle, or about further solidifying an old dysfunctional one?

One thing I see often is that folks will intend a retreat to function as a kickstart, a jumpstart to or of a new way of being, and then are surprised when indeed it does not, are surprised when it is difficult to maintain gains from the retreat in daily life.

This contrast can exacerbate embarrassment, shame, disappointment. Bad feelings about the space between what was and what is; a briefly achieved fantasy of good feeling shatters and we are where we were. Always striving, failing, falling short. The cycle repeats.

Sometimes something can happen on retreat that we bring back with us. We might learn something new, try something new. We may come back home with medicines. Medicine in this sense is not just a concoction we imbibe like a pill; it is food for the soul, it is nourishing. It may be herbal, it may not be. It may be a realization, a wisdom, a mantra, a meditation, a shock to the system, a successful risk taken, a slow burn that we can't quite put our finger on. But we may come back changed.

Sometimes this shaking up is exactly the medicine our system, our soul, our body, needs. Sometimes we don't know that thing until it hits us, until it sweeps away, until it cleanses our system like a sudden cold shower, rinsing away what no longer serves us. Sometimes this happens at home. Sometimes it doesn't. I respect the need, the feeling, the impetus, to try something new, something not-yet-tried (by us). To risk. But I find that people who move and travel to find themselves rarely do find themselves elsewhere. Wherever you go, there you are.

What does/can it mean to face ourselves, as we are, right now, here?

Of course, sometimes we may need a change of scenery in support of our mental health, but if we only can maintain some semblance of mental health or connection to spirituality when we are 'on retreat', this can be a dangerous relegation of the spiritual to 'the elsewhere', authenticity and home to 'the elsewhere', something that is always out of reach, never home, never in our own body, never where we are. Always not here. The grass is greener.

When we travel – physically, mentally, emotionally – we encounter spirituality in different ways, in different forms and incarnations; the home that is our body already is always in a process of going through changes. With different stimulus, our shape changes; maybe the familiar body becomes unusual, looks different. To borrow a phrase from Sara Ahmed, we become a '(strange) stranger' in our own flesh. To become strange to ourselves can become a moment of teaching, of learning; a moment of risk; to become closer to home through realizing our own otherness, we (be)come home.

I'll relate this, just for a moment, to my other love – tarot. The tarot's retreater is, of course, the Hermit. One thing I love about the Hermit card is that while it signifies solitude and retreat for the purpose of gaining new knowledge, the flame of enlightenment is really what sits inside of us – it is our own inner fire there all along, keeping us warm, leading us to be better versions of ourselves, if only we listen in and connect. Sometimes it is just shutting the doors to many other babblings to give us the time and space and resonance to hear ourselves once again.

A beauty of the Hermit is in its strong reminder that we often don't need to go anywhere else to do this, to connect, to change, to transform. The lamp of change is already inside us, leading the way. We may just have to polish it a bit, to let the light shine through.

chapter Six

Human Connection

FINDING ~~██~~ AND BUILDING COMMUNITIES

Humans! Wherever there's humans, there's trouble – that is, hurt feelings, group dysfunction, drama, disagreements, and everything in between.

Of course, there's another side to this – when we make time for genuine and authentic connection with our fellow human beings, beautiful things can happen. Community care, mutual aid, love (whether it be romantic, platonic, or familial), feeling as though we truly belong, as though others understand us, will be there for us, and will help provide for us no matter what. As much as I may have some deep-down skepticism about the trials and tribulations of connecting with people in any type of group setting, I also know these spaces can be infinitely beautiful, despite their challenges.

Humans are social animals – we thrive with one another. For most of us, our mental health is greatly improved when we have access to loving touch, unyielding compassion and support – when we feel we are not alone in the trials and tribulations of existence, when we are accepted no matter where we've been or what we've done. Fantasies of unconditional love can be lovely, but the fact of the matter is, for many of us, love is conditional; relationship is conditional, and for adults, that's healthy. I'm in relationship with the folks in my life on the condition they treat me with respect and care.

This may seem a bit of an off-base criticism of folks seeking spiritual community, but hear me out. I find that sometimes, people seek to belong to a spiritual group, where they can look up to a spiritual leader who has all of the answers to solving all their problems – they're looking for a substitute for one or both of their parents. I'm not a psychologist or therapist or anything like that, but/and I have noticed the unintentional transference that does sometimes happen in people seeking to heal themselves by belonging to some kind of spiritual community.

I get it – my own childhood left a lot to be desired, and my parents neglected and abandoned me; I never felt loved or cared for by them. I know how deeply painful it can be, and how sometimes absolutely impossible it feels to heal from something so heavy – especially when the common discourse seems to be, "I'm sure it's not that bad," "just let it go, they're family, nothing's more important than family," or even worse, the insinuations that child victims and survivors are to blame for our parents' inability to love us.

It's hard. I know. For me, a significant part of this journey has been learning to become my own loving parent: my own loving mother, my own loving father. On Mother's Day, after spending years being depressed and miserable, I learned to honour myself for being my own mother. I did the same for myself on Father's Day, appreciating the ways I've fathered myself, too, over the years. What has this looked like? Oh, geeze – so many different ways. Sometimes, it's looked like getting myself a cute stuffed animal from the dollar store to hug in bed when I'm upset – a comfort I always wished for as a kid. It's meant hugging myself, when no one else would. It's meant talking myself down from the cliff where the bad thoughts are, away from that place of feeling insignificant, unworthy, ugly, and unlovable. It's meant ordering myself some food when I've had a bad day, getting an extra blanket for my bed. Being my own loving parent has meant, well, loving myself – and relying on myself when the going gets tough.

For many people, they've got their parents or family as unwavering support through thick and thin. I know loads of people who talk to their parents nearly every day about every little thing in their lives; who have their parents to bounce off the big decisions of life, who affirm them on the daily. For many folks, that's unwavering, their guiding light, a flame that won't ever go out.

I've never had that. Friendships, though strong and meaningful, sometimes become wrong-sized. The same can be said for romantic relationships. My constant, then, has been me.

Maybe the same is true for you – maybe you haven't had much support, and you've had to learn to love yourself and support yourself through it all. Many people live complex lives and come from complex stories, complex pasts. Many of us are a whole mess – and, hey, some of the time that's definitely me!

Whenever I go for a walk it fills me with wonder and curiosity that everyone I pass has a galaxy within them – a lifetime of loves, losses, joys and pains.

When we experience pains, loss, wounding – our impetus, often, is to heal. Spirituality is one big pillar that folks lean on. And spirituality is powerful. Those of you familiar with my work will know I've talked for years about how magic and witchcraft and animism and spirit work and all that have grounded me and held me tight when nothing else could; I can genuinely say that magic and witchcraft gave me my whole life, and that I would not be here today without it. My spirituality has helped save my life more than once; my spirituality has given me life.

Sometimes when we are seeking healing, we are vulnerable.

Sometimes, that vulnerability is taken advantage of, and people in need of a genuine pick-me-up end up in a high-demand group or cult. Yikes! Or, more mundanely and more commonly, sometimes we're so upset or wonky feeling and so unaware of the extent of our own trauma and feelings and triggers that we lash out at everyone around us, even those who mean well – or, in the desperation to connect, we latch onto leaders and groups who may not be abusive, but may cause us to become even more confused and unsure of who we are and what our path is.

It may sound like I'm being a bit of a bitch here. You might be reading this thinking, "What the hell, Sabrina. I'm just here to learn witchcraft. And now you're telling me that I need to do some corny bullshit like hug myself and be my own loving parent? What are you smoking, and can I have some?"

I'm not joking, and I'm not smoking anything!

Magic is amazing. Witchcraft is wonderful.

For me, this is an entire way of life. I have never been able to separate all of this magic stuff, this spirit stuff, this witchy animist stuff, from every moment of every day that I'm alive.

I gain so much from my relationship with the clouds, the rain, the sun, the snow, the downtown skyscrapers, the beach, my bundles of incense, the antique wood my altar is made of, my saint statues, the roses on my bedside table, my ancestor spirits, the snacks in my fridge, my collection of candles and herbs and bath salts and and and. The spirits of the land. My bed. They hold me, just the same. I am always with them, held, in community, in magic.

And, and, and: I still believe from the bottom of my heart that it is so important that I know how to hold myself, to soothe myself; to know my history, to know what wounds and strengths I carry with me today from my family, dead and alive, to know how they have touched me, made me strong and talented and also made me fucked up and confused. To the extent that it's possible, in this practice, in engaging with spiritual community, in magic making, it's so important to at least begin to try to face ourselves, to look at and understand where we've been, what wounds are still raw, and what's being healed. To know what we're susceptible to, what our triggers are, what our nasty unhelpful patterns are, to know what those nasty thoughts are, and what we can and want to replace them with instead.

What does this have to do with witchcraft?

Y'all wanna do magic, right?

Well, it's this deep diving inner work – what some folks call 'shadow work,' though I don't personally resonate with that framing – that will help you have the grounding and frame of reference and/or mind to determine what type of ritual should be done when, what spiritual group to get involved with when, if at all.

Instead of a spell to get back a lover who has strayed, how about some spell work on yourself to increase your self love and what you believe you deserve, and what you believe is possible for you? How about boosting your feelings of worthiness? What about some protection work to strengthen your own boundaries with magic? What about doing a banishing or cord cutting, or even just a simple ritual of mourning, release, and laying it all to rest?

Who we are, where we're at with ourselves, has a huge role in how we approach magic and witchcraft – what type of workings we do, and whether or not they're actually effective and impactful.

Whenever I'm doing spell work consultations with women whose partners have cheated, it's interesting how few of them have gone down the route of thinking about/reflecting on their worthiness, if they're accepting crumbs and confusing it for a whole meal (and if so, why), if they've got limiting beliefs in what they feel is possible for them, not to mention the confusion about why the hell we'd even wanna be with someone who we gotta put a spell on to catch.

You know what, no judgement – I've been there. I've done it. It was unpleasant as hell, I got what I wanted, it was the worst relationship of my life, and I learned my lesson. And now here I am to share it all with you, so you can learn from my mistakes!

When we have that self-reflection, facing your demons, knowing yourself, thing I was talking about before, our whole approach to magic changes. Our way of being in spiritual community also changes, as does what we want from it, other people, and how we show up there, our expectations, how we deal with conflict, whether our behaviour is elevated or petty, etc.

This is not about me trying to prove that I'm more woke or enlightened or healed than anyone else. That's not the point. I'm so happy with what I've achieved in my healing of so many things, and I know I have quite a few more paths to walk on my road to healing and peace. But/and, this process of knowing ourselves and becoming ourselves, uncovering roots and planting new seeds, is a lifelong journey. It's one that never ends, that I recommit myself to every day, with joy.

The more we can ground and root into ourselves – our own sense of self, of home, of our own values, the better we'll be able to withstand any conflict or weirdness that does arise, whether in ourselves as individuals, or when we come into encounters with others.

Seeking Connection

Humans need connection.

Well, I'm pretty sure everyone, everything, all beings, need connection – none of us are islands, and even islands are actually multifaceted ecosystems of many, many different beings (animal, vegetable, mineral, and more) coming together to create and be something unique and special. We are all networked, interconnected – assemblages, entanglements.

Even our bodies are made up of so many other bodies – our organs, our cells, the water we drink, the food we eat, the air we breathe. To exist at all is to always already be collaborating/in a process of collaboration, connection, and dialogue. I even wrote a whole book about that – it's called *Witchbody*. In it, I talk a lot about how the interconnectedness of all beings, how we are always already touching and influencing one another, and how magic and witchcraft can help us see collaborations in all areas of life and existence, past the realm of witchery and the materiality of the spiritual.

And while I absolutely adore a philosophical deep dive – and need to acknowledge that finding community among spirits and non-human beings is a big part of why I'm alive and thriving today – going to that place is not the purpose of this little section. One of those books has been published, and the other is in the process of being created. Today, here, right now, in this book, I'm zooming out a bit, and talking about actual, literal human connection. The relationships we as humans have between ourselves and other humans. There really isn't any substitute for it, and human connection is something we all do need in order to have longer, happier, healthier lives.

It pains me to say it – as someone who has maybe spent too much time being overly independent – but research from a lot of different spheres has shown that the healthier and stronger our relationships, the longer, healthier lives we tend to live. Anyone familiar with studies of trauma and healing has likely heard of the ACE score – a list of 'adverse childhood experiences' which ranges from bad to terrible. Higher ACE scores tend to correlate with more health concerns later in life. Folks in healthy long-term relationships also tend to report better health, and longer lives. These statistics were sobering to me once I learned of them, and were a bit of a reality check that I'd need, at some point, to let my walls down and take the risk to let people in – for my own health.

Community is a common place where humans seek – and find – connection. These can be affinity groups or clubs, through playing sports or working out together, jamming together as musicians, or even something spiritual, like going to church, temple, or meditation classes.

It's super common to feel the pull towards community – both in general, but especially when we're going through a tough time, a liminal space where we're in transition from one part of our story to the next.

Folks turn to spirituality for so many reasons, which may include but are not limited to: seeking to understand the world we live in, both material and immaterial, and our place in it; to feel less alone; to feel accepted for who we are, in all our certainty and uncertainty; looking for a new hobby or social circle; seeking to understand the self more; to feel a sense of release and trust about our own lives; and also to feel more empowered and in control of our own lives.

I get it, I've been there! And sometimes, when we're going through something – maybe something painful, challenging, or chaotic – we may be particularly desperate for community, for connection. And there's absolutely nothing wrong with that! Sometimes a wobbly community, or a new community we haven't fully vetted or checked out yet, can help us feel less alone and get through tough times.

However, sometimes, when we've just been through something intense, and we're reaching out for connection, some people or groups might seek to take advantage of our vulnerability, and use that to harm or exploit us even further.

If we're feeling vulnerable, this is often the absolute last thing we need.

People have tried this type of vampiric exploitation on me, too – it's weird, and it's a serious problem in life in general, and spiritual communities aren't exempt from this, unfortunately. I know it may be a bit of a bummer to read this, and maybe it takes the air out of your balloon – but my intention in writing this book is to be real, to be blunt, to be authentic to my experience, and to speak from integrity. I would not feel as though I was doing my duty to myself, and to newer practitioners especially, if I didn't at least include some words of warning and wariness here – not because I think you can't figure it out yourself, but because I wish someone had sat me down and told me all of this twenty years ago, when I first started to seriously dig into the overlap between spirituality and community.

The Desperation to Connect

Closeness and connection is so important to human beings, that we often try to find and maintain connections at nearly any cost – the idea that it's better to be attached and unhappy, than simply unattached (and, by proxy, either unsupported or less supported). Connection, even when at times unpleasant (unhappy at best, abusive at worst), can feel like a lifeline – having someone to rely on can feel like the difference between life and death, whether or not it is.

What I'm trying to say here is that while connection can be beautiful, and incredibly important – sometimes we ignore red flags, or even conveniently push them under the rug. I've done it! Sometimes being alone can feel like it might be a kind of death. And humans tend to have a pretty intact drive to survive, to live – at all costs. So, staving off loneliness can feel like the best way to maintain proximity to our own aliveness.

Connection is beautiful. It can feel amazing to fuse with another, whether it's through romantic love, sex, friendship, a spiritual or other community group. Sometimes, though, that fusion either isn't healthy, disconnects us from our sense of self, or both. Sometimes, the desperation to connect can cause us to disregard our judgement, our feelings, our intuition, and our needs. This is important to keep in mind as we encounter and build relationships with others, particularly in the context of spiritual community.

Healing and Harm in Spiritual Communities

Unfortunately, spirituality is a space that many people go to find healing, and sometimes just find their traumas or harms exacerbated – and occcasionally, they walk away with new ones.

I'm still in the process of doing more in-depth research on the connections between healing and harm in spiritual communities, but one thing that I've found particularly disturbing is when someone is a genuinely talented medium or spiritual worker, and uses those talents to manipulate or maliciously shape their students and community members. Or, in some circumstances, folks are just talented con artists, and sometimes even very intelligent, well-adjusted people find themselves taken in by the con.

For the sake of example, I'd like to share a fairly minimal but still very shitty personal experience. In an online business space I was in, I made a vulnerable post. Someone reached out to me in response. As I'm a spiritual worker myself, I was just looking for collegiality, friendship, and kinship – and, hey, I'm not above buying a reading from a fellow worker sometimes!

I had a bad feeling about this person, which I ignored (to my slight peril), thinking maybe I was just on my default setting of 'judgemental bitch' – she called me and we had a weird but generally nice chat; she told me a few spiritual things about my situation that were pretty spot on. She then emailed me, telling me that she "knew" that my soul "wanted and needed to enter into a spiritual coaching relationship" with her, that it was the only way to remove any blockages and clear my path for the next steps on my journey. It was "divinely aligned," and, hey, she was in direct contact with my soul, and apparently my soul already said yes, so who was I to say no?

Well, I did say no – and after she harassed me on a few different social media platforms, tried to guilt-trip me into giving her a testimonial for our chat (testimonial for what, exactly? I'm still not sure), I said no again, and decided to just let her have the last word – which was that she could now see who I "really am," that she "knows the sad truth" about me – and I blocked her. While this is a small example, and I'm not traumatized by it, this kind of thing is a tiny example of what I do often see in spiritual communities. To say it's inappropriate would be an understatement.

So, what's the problem here? Not coaching – hell, I offer mentorships myself, and have been more than happy to pay talented teachers the big bucks to further my own education, spiritual or otherwise.

The problem here is that this person observed me in a moment of vulnerability, and saw me as a mark.

I have my own business, so I understand the need to make money, pay the bills, and grow – but I would never in a million years tell someone that I know them better than they know themselves, and I'd never dream of telling someone that I know exactly what their soul wants (and that it's to send a few thousand dollars my way).

I do have offerings in that price range – but my philosophy is that whether or not folks want to make that type of investment in their own spiritual growth and learning – with me, nonetheless – is fully their decision. They know what's best for them. Would I love to have folks in my courses? Do I know they'll benefit? Totally. Do I know my courses and teachings change lives? Yes, I do, people tell me that all the time, and have for years. But, I don't presume to know what anyone's soul wants, and even if I did… isn't it kinda weird to pressure someone like that, after connecting in vulnerability?

This woman did what many folks in the spiritual industry unfortunately do – attempted to take my agency away from me, and put it solely with her. She presented herself as having a superior insight into my soul's desires, and suggested that the only way I could level up was through dependence on her instead. This is a really disempowering way to view spirituality, as well as any relationship between student and teacher, coach and client.

What's the difference between that and what I do? Well, I don't think I'm the only teacher out there. I love what I do, I believe in my work, and I know I'm not for everyone. I don't want to create our encourage any unhealthy dependency on me – I'd rather create incubation spaces, whether one-on-one or in a group, where I can ask questions and lead conversations in such a way that whoever I'm working with sees the power and agency within themselves – that's always been there. I'd like folks to feel more connected to themselves and the world around them – knowing their own power, their own ability to change their own circumstances, and being able to connect with and mobilize their own power.

Enough about me though – let's bring this back to you, and why I'm telling you this right now. Do I think you're too stupid to pick up on sketchy people? No, I most certainly do not! However, even folks with good judgement and strong intuition can sometimes hop on calls with folks looking to exploit our weaknesses – hey, it happened to me. It pains me to think about how many folks this lady's schtick must have worked on. That's not what I want from the spiritual community, but sadly that's sometimes what it looks like.

There's a lot of folks in this space working under the label of 'healer' – and this has always made me feel uncomfortable. Maybe it's just a hangover from my childhood experience in Spiritualism, where even acts of energy healing were framed as forms of mediumship – people could be successful or unsuccessful mediums, but the act of 'healing' was framed as an act of being a channel or conduit. The human being isn't the 'healer,' Spirit is – the human is just a medium, a vessel for the expression of spirit(s), and so the term 'healer' was very rarely used. It was always acknowledged that the healing power was in Spirit (or God, or spirits, or The Divine Universe), not in the human being themselves (though the skill of a medium was always acknowledged).

I'm not comfortable positioning myself as a healer because I'm not the one who is doing the healing, even if someone feels 'healed' or like they are carrying a lighter burden after a session with me. I serve my client and the spirits by creating an incubation space, a container, for magic and transformation to happen. My goal is to help my clients see that they are their own best healers, their own authority figures, their own spiritual teachers. Yes, I am good at what I do, but there are ways of framing that that can cause clients to feel helpless, desperate, powerless, ineffectual, disempowered, and reliant on you. That's not a healthy relationship for anyone to be in.

Of course, the extreme end of this is the cult, or high demand group. Many scholars and writers have written about this. One interesting yogic case study is written by Matthew Remski, who leans very heavily on the excellent work of Alexandra Stein, who, in her book *Terror, Love, and Brainwashing*, applies John Bowlby's attachment theory (which has grown countless legs since his original contribution, becoming common ways of understanding child-parent relationships as well as love relationships between romantically involved adults) to cults and totalist high demand groups.

Stein writes that there is actually no common starting attachment style (there are three organized – secure, anxious, and avoidant, and one that is simply called disorganized) among individuals who become involved in cults, but that cults' success – and the difficulty of leaving them – is much like why it becomes challenging for so many victims to leave abusive relationships: cults create disorganized attachment in their adherents. Stein describes disorganized attachment as involving a mix of love and terror – the primary caregiver and attachment figure, on which one relies for love, affection, and care, is also a source of terror due to an infliction of pain, harm, shame, or other form of violence. I won't get into the science of this, but the short version is that this combination makes it very difficult for people to leave.

What a terrible state to end up in, when all we're trying to do is heal ourselves, and connect with the grounding power of spirituality!

Oftentimes, the beginning of involvement in high-demand groups and groups that are healthy and healing can look similar – group members or leaders may be kind, welcoming, accepting. I'm not suggesting we all freak out and set our settings to high alert at all times – how exhausting would that be! What I am trying to say here is that not everyone will have your best interests at heart, even though we're talking about specifically spiritual community. And, yes, this is sadly true for witchy community, too.

Just because you've found a group with rules and codes of conduct doesn't mean you've found a cult, and just because a leader questions you, calls you out on something, challenges you, or disagrees with you doesn't mean that person is abusive. This is where that self-knowledge comes in – knowing what's yours, and what's theirs – having an awareness of our own triggers can be really helpful here in discerning what's what.

Here are some questions you might want to ask yourself:

- Do I feel like this spiritual teacher is helping me connect more to myself, or do I feel more mistrustful of myself and who I am and want to be? Do I feel more or less connected to myself?
- Does this person try to convince me that they know what I want better than I do?
- How is the person with boundaries? How do they react when I communicate my own boundaries, around little things or big things?
- Do they make me feel more vulnerable, or more empowered?
- Do I feel more connected to my own agency, or more disengaged from it?
- Am I pressured to prematurely share intimate parts of my life and past, such as trauma and abuse information?
- Am I being asked to give up my name, and choose a new name?
- Am I being told that the spiritual group or teacher is more important than anything else in my life?
- Am I being told not to question the person in charge? How are my questions received?
- Am I being asked to step away or distance from friends, family, and/or other people I go to for comfort and support?
- Is the group more important than school, work, or self-care? If so, why? Is that coming from me, or the teacher/leader?
- Am I somehow feeling a craving to give up my power and agency and decision-making processes, and give full control over my life and my choices to someone else?
- What is my role in this connection and this relational learning experience? Am I taking responsibility for myself and my choices, or am I putting all of the blame for my shortcomings and failures on someone else? Am I in a habit of - and do I enjoy - giving my power and agency away to others? What benefit do I get from this behaviour (ie, does it make me feel like a loved child to entrust all choices to someone else)?

The Difficulties of Spiritual Leadership

Being in a leadership position is intense! And, in spiritual community in particular, everything can get a little more complex. Why? Well, this seems to be due to the myriad of reasons people tend to turn towards spiritual seeking – in times of crisis or distress or vulnerability, many people seek healing, answers, community, and acceptance. Dipping toes into spirituality is often free or low-cost – just the price of a book like the ones you have in your hands right now, whether you purchased it yourself, borrowed it from a friend, or got it from the library. Many spiritual leaders and teachers are ultimately interested in being of service – myself included. Yes, I do have higher ticket courses and programs, as do many other spiritual teachers – thorough education ain't always free!

Going to church or reading a few books on witchcraft, though, is a lot cheaper (read: more accessible) than years or even decades of therapy. Add on other professional services such as psychiatry, naturopathy, yoga or other movement classes as ways of shaking trauma out of the body – all of these things cost money, and can take time to bear results. I've been seeing my current therapist for about seven or eight years now, and it's only recently that I've graduated to seeing him monthly rather than weekly or bi-weekly. I'm thankful as hell to him, but/and therapy can be a slow burn, and costly.

What I'm trying to say is that sometimes people go to spirituality or witchcraft or magic for things they would be more likely to get through a mix of other healing modalities, including talk therapy. It's not an either/or – magic and my spiritual practice have definitely saved my life – but I do feel that when folks are not right with themselves, and/or have no interest in being so, they can approach spiritual spaces in general and magic in particular with attitudes of immediacy, entitlement, and a lack of personal responsibility and self-awareness.

As someone who has ended up in positions of spiritual leadership somewhat by accident – this was never my goal, but I've been told I'm good at it, so here we are – I've seen this come into play in my professional practice. I've had folks come to me as they might a parent, looking for me to validate their every feeling. I've gotten novels from folks with no boundaries, sending uninvited litanies of trauma, as though now that I, the spiritual teacher, have held it in my social media inbox, they can now be freed, absolved, purified.

As a spiritual leader and teacher, I'm put into the position of professional problem-solver – and, to be honest, I absolutely love working in this capacity. It seems to be a big part of what I was born to do.

That being said, I once had a client who was convinced I was the reincarnation of her dead daughter. I've had completely unhinged ex-clients harass me on multiple platforms, for no real reason – all of our readings were absolutely great, I just didn't reply to their oversharing chatty DMs about their life in between, which apparently made me a demon. Oops! What does this mean? Perhaps unavoidably, some folks will, often unbeknownst to them, have an experience of transference with you.

What's transference? Let me tell you!

I'll illustrate this all with an example: in the context of me building a relationship with my therapist, part of the reason that relationship works and has been healing to me is because my therapist has been a reliable, kind, affirmative stand-in for my non-existent relationship with my parents; as a kid, they were not stable attachment figures, and treated me with a mix of disdain, neglect, displeasure, disappointment, and sometimes nicely.

Not having any ability to predict what I'd experience from my parents, my attachment system got fucked up and my brain got wired in a fucked up way, giving me the worst form of attachment (disorganized, when figures of love/caregivers are also objects of fear and terror), and Complex Post Traumatic Stress Disorder (CPTSD). Having my therapist give me more or less the same, reliable, caring version of himself every time I've seen him has enabled me to learn to build what's called earned secure attachment.

Until the process was kinda complete – I'm able to form secure attachments now, and accurately assess who that might be possible with – I had no clue that process was happening. My therapist did, obviously, since he's good at what he does and he had the long game in mind. That was a big part of the point of therapy, for me, even though I didn't know it when I started – to learn to not feel fucking crazy all the time, I needed to learn to move from disorganized attachment, the worst kind, to secure, the most healthy and stable. I, unbeknownst to myself, had transference with my therapist, and as a result of his thoughtful engagement with me about this, used that transference to heal me.

As I've spoken with my therapist and others in the psychotherapy and psychoanalytic industries about what I do, I've learned that there are three professions in which transference is most likely to occur in are among therapists, teachers, and leaders or public figures. Interestingly, being in a position of spiritual leadership often in some way encompasses elements of all three of these roles (though, of course, it needs to be said – not any accredited or regulated form of psychotherapy of the type I'm describing as having done with my therapist.) While I don't have any complaints that the spiritual industry isn't regulated, I appreciate very much that if my therapist were to fuck up severely or mistreat or violate me, I would have some regulatory board to appeal to in order to advocate for myself as a patient. I've never engaged in this type of complaint making process, so I'm sure there are similar challenges there as many I've known have experienced in the legal system, trying to get justice for violence.

While part of my doctoral research has included research into psychology, cults, and group dynamics, and I've done a lot of reading on trauma, attachment, family systems, and relationships as a crucial point of my own healing, I'm not trained in any official capacity in anything psychological. I'm not a therapist, I'm not a psychologist, I'm not accredited in any of those things, and it would be deeply irresponsible for me to misrepresent myself as such. In all of my in-depth teaching materials, I make it very clear to my students that I very much believe spirituality and magic are only some parts of a larger puzzle of overall spiritual, emotional, physical, and mental wellness; it doesn't make someone less of a witch to go to therapy every week. I know that the services I provide, while valuable, are no substitute for regular sessions with licensed mental health professionals. Similarly, there's no substitute for a deep spiritual practice, either. They are simply not the same thing.

That being said, the research I have done into these topics has enriched my own approach to spiritual leadership and spiritual teaching, and what's at stake when one is in a position of leadership, either by choice or by circumstance. I now know that some people will transfer onto me their issues with people in their life – maybe parents or other authority figures, or even the ex best-friend who they kinda love and kinda hate and just want to yell at, or their sibling who they've always had a weird relationship with.

This does make me take stuff a little less personally when it does happen, and it's also helped me walk as softly as possible in this role and move with an awareness that it might be happening for folks I work with, and how to point it out and/or mitigate it when it comes up.

If I'm giving someone what I perceive to be gentle, constructive criticism in a group setting, and they have an emotional meltdown as a result, it's a sign to me that they may have some unresolved issues around criticism, perhaps from parents or caregivers. It's not an opportunity for me to psychoanalyze someone and shame them for their response, but to hold them in the truth of whatever they are experiencing, and to gently guide them back to the present moment, and, if possible, suggest some other resources they might also turn to, to better understand and process what came up for them in that moment of activation. This doesn't come up for me often, but if you're in a position of spiritual leadership, I do believe things like this are a numbers game and only a matter of time. It's possible to handle these situations with kindness, care, compassion, and acceptance, and appreciation to/for/of the student for being with themselves authentically in that moment.

However, I'm aware that not all of you reading this will be interested in taking up the mantle of spiritual teaching or leadership. The stuff I've mentioned above are those things that don't often get talked about or addressed when folks talk about wanting to be spiritual leaders – it isn't just knowing magic, there's so much more to it!

If you're someone with no interest in occupying a leadership role, and are more interested in simply finding a good teacher or group to practice with, I would recommend doing your own self-reflection work to sort out what leadership in this capacity means to you and why. Are you looking for that all-loving parental figure, either consciously or subconsciously? Have you been going through a shitty time, and are you feeling maybe a little bit too open-minded? Maybe to the extent that your brain falls out of your head and onto the floor?

The transference thing I talked about above is huge – and there are countless stories of people in positions of spiritual leadership abusing their positions of authority. Alexandra Stein in her book *Terror, Love, and Brainwashing* innovatively applies John Bowlby's attachment theory to understand how people get roped into cults or high-demand groups: basically, by the creation of disorganized attachment, often in people who hadn't previously had that attachment style. Abusive spiritual leaders create experiences of intimacy and vulnerability, and alternate excessive displays of love with cruel punishment. Followers become wired to seek out the leader's love and approval, even in the face of mistreatment. If you've been paying attention to the news at all in the last while, I'm sure you're aware of the horrors of NXIVM, covered widely over the last few years; and Netflix's popular docuseries *Wild Wild Country* outlines the rise and fall of Bhagwan Sri Rajneesh's cult during his lifetime.

Add onto that the age of social media and parasocial relationships. Originally used to describe the general public's bizarre relationship to celebrities – feeling like they know them very well and are best pals, when in reality the celeb has absolutely no idea who they are – now it's increasingly used to describe the one-sided relationships and projections that happen between social media content creators and their followers or fans. If you're more of a consumer than a creator, it can be especially important to be aware of projections, fantasies, and assumptions about people outside of our direct social circles.

While I do think spiritual leaders and teachers who really do wish to be responsible with the power they have would benefit to be aware of all these types of dynamics, it is also my wish that spiritual seekers also come to their practice with some self-awareness as to their own situations, to the extent that it's possible – bad patterns, traumas, whatever.

This is so tough, since folks come to spirituality to heal – but/and I wonder if sometimes too much pressure is put on spiritual leaders to be a grab-bag of everything. Stand-in parent, stand-in therapist, stand-in best friend. This blurriness doesn't benefit anyone, and it especially doesn't benefit the seeker or student! There's nothing wrong with becoming friends with our teachers – hell, I've done it myself – but/and, what I've come to refer to as 'pedestal culture' is very much a thing, and whether you dream of becoming a teacher or happy to be a lifelong learner never taking up the mantle of instructor, it's an important dynamic to be aware of.

What is this pedestal culture? Well, it's simple: when we put those we admire on a pedestal, we elevate them above all other people. We live by their word, we love everything they say and do and are, they can do no wrong, we are sometimes obsessed and just love and adore them completely. We expect them to be all knowing, all loving, and always right. This is cute in theory I guess, but in reality, it's a nightmare of dehumanization and objectification. When we put people on pedestals and expect 24/7 perfection – yes, even people in positions of leadership and power – we rob them of their humanity, of their ability to just be, breathe, live life, make mistakes, learn from them. What's put on a pedestal can only fall off of it, and often smashes to pieces. I've seen some people try to do this to me in the past; the only violent hate mail I've ever gotten has been from folks who at one point sent me the most effusive love letters.

There's one in particular I remember – I had a tarot reading booked on the day of the attempted coup at the US Capitol building. Though I live in Canada now, I grew up in the United States, and feel very American; the United States will always be home to me. Watching the violence on the news, I felt deeply sick – physically, mentally, emotionally. I had never seen anything like it before. I'm not a nationalist by any means, but I still felt crazy to see what was happening. I was in no state to do anything, let alone read cards. I kindly messaged my client to reschedule, both out of respect for her as well as for myself – and what followed was a stream of vitriol – demeaning and insulting me as a person, essays about how disappointed she was in who I "really" am, which is so "different" from my "online persona" – forwarding my messages to friends, I asked – was I being a bitch here? The unanimous opinion was that I was actually being way too nice.

While that experience fucking sucked – and I've only explained the tip of the iceberg – it led me to reflect on this tendency of some folks to put leaders and teachers on a pedestal, disallowing us from simple human experiences and feelings, like sickness or overwhelm. It was instructive to me in that it helped me learn the extent to which some folks project on those they idealize, idolize, and look up to. I vow to never behave like this to another person.

So, whether you're a spiritual leader, wanna be a spiritual leader, or are looking for one, please, I beg of you: remember we are all just human beings, people, having a topsy turvy wild experience of this thing called life. I do actually believe I have a lot of things sorted out – today, anyway – but/and, I have a lot of things to learn still, and I'm sure that my ideas may change over time or at least become more nuanced, as I gain in both years and experience. I can only share what's worked for me, and help lead those who work with me and learn from me back to themselves.

This wariness of guru culture, pedestal culture, idolization culture that we sometimes see perpetuated both by teachers and students/followers, has deepened my resolve to teach from this place: I am not your healer, I am not your absolution, I am not your one and only answer; it may be corny or tacky or both to cite Tony Robbins – but his documentary is called "I am not your guru." I love that phrase; I really believe it. As a spiritual teacher, I see my role as being about reminding you of your agency, your power, your sovereignty, your own wisdom. I don't want to create dependence in anyone who works with me – I don't want anyone to feel that they are wobbly in their spiritual practice unless they're copying me, doing what I'm doing, regurgitating my ideas. Spiritual leadership, for me, ain't about creating clones of myself – but about creating containers and pathways for those who work with me to find their own personal leadership in themselves, to find the answers and knowledge that is always already deep inside your soul, your being, waiting to be found, waiting to blossom.

If I have any advice for the leaders of tomorrow, it's to be ready for everything under the sun.

If I have any advice for folks who just wanna chill out and learn, with no desire to lead – it would be to make sure you remember your teachers are just people – they pee every day, eat food, sometimes get headaches; sometimes they swear and get into arguments with their partners. Sometimes they get sick, sometimes they drink wine. This doesn't make them less worth learning from.

And also, in seeking the spiritual, don't abandon yourself; remember to keep that inner flame burning bright. If you're unsure how to proceed, check in with your gut. Not everyone is for everyone. That doesn't mean someone is evil or abusive – just that not everyone is compatible.

RESPONSIBILITY, ETHICS, AND HARM

Responsibility can feel like a hot potato – nobody wants to take it; it's always passed to someone else! Taking responsibility for harming others isn't always an easy thing to do, though it is a necessary aspect of healthy, happy relationships – and it's a part of community and group dynamics, too.

It can be challenging navigating dynamics of healing and harm, especially when it can feel easiest to throw responsibility onto someone else for our own hurts. My perspective here is multifaceted – I believe it's important for folks who cause harm to acknowledge their impact, and I also feel it's crucial for aggrieved parties to take a look at their own role in contributing to harmful dynamics (this could be around unhealthy choices, uncontrolled triggers, trauma histories that jolt into the foreground, etc). I don't mean victim blaming, at all. Just that victims and survivors often need to come to terms with how their warning bells may be broken - and repair them. Do we need to always heal from all of our hurts in order to go into community, into relationship? Definitely not – healing and integration can often happen in community, in relationship. Relationships can heal us, can teach us.

And so my perspective here isn't black and white. I'm not saying folks have to be perfectly well-mannered, nice-at-all-times people with absolutely zero triggers or trauma, in order to be unleashed into the world to play with others. We all have our own stories, our own trials and tribulations, our own issues to move through, our own joys, goals, and unique awe-filled moments. When people come together, harm is pretty unavoidable. The question is, how is it dealt with? As a team, or as enemies? With an open heart, with curiosity, with a trying to uncover, to understand? Or with cruelty?

Ethics can look different in each moment, in each situation. Ethical behaviour (treating yourself with love, with care, with respect) can look like divesting from a person, group, or situation. It can also look like persistence, patience, repair, taking responsibility, even when we don't want to. Conversations around harm are never comfortable, but in long-standing relationships they're unavoidable. This is true, too, when it comes to interpersonal group dynamics.

Benefits and Drawbacks of Group Practice

Group practice, like any other thing on this earth, has its own benefits and drawbacks. You may start off loving it, and later decide to go it alone, or vice versa.

Group practice can be fantastic if you're an extrovert and love other people. I found in some of the witchy groups I spent time in, there was actually a lot more hours spent cooking, eating, and socializing than doing magic or talking about esoteric spiritual philosophies. This may suit some people really well! If you're happy to give full control over to others – and you find folks who you can trust to hold that power well – groups may also be a good fit. Not all groups and leaders are deserving of trust – but when you find one that is, it can be a truly cathartic experience. In a good, experienced, healthy and open group, you might meet fantastic people who can help guide your growth. Having folks around to bond over faith, and to troubleshoot magical happenings with, can be really grounding for some folks.

However, there's a chance you might find a group that doesn't have your best interests at heart, or takes advantage of your enthusiasm and newness to the practice, to guide you in a direction that you don't yet know isn't either above board, or the only way to do things. You can always leave a group, but I've heard many stories from newer folks who didn't know that they were in a weird situation – they just thought all groups were like that. Group practice can also be a bit discouraging in terms of developing personal spiritual philosophy, and personal spiritual voice. The creative and innovator in me could never be happy being in a witchy group not of my own design.

Solitary practice can, at times, be a bit lonely and socially isolating – but I love that it gives me the space to focus on myself, to reflect on my own philosophies, ideas, and inclinations – to troubleshoot, try new things, and innovate. Over the years, through a lot of trial and error, I've built trust in myself and my spirit team, as well as in my own knowledge and execution of energy work and magic. This can encourage creative thought – after all, the big magical names we all know, both historical and contemporary, were daring and bold in their magic, in being unafraid to do something new and to speak about it.

It's not an either-or choice, though – many who are in a group, also have a solitary practice. And many who practice alone may participate in vibrant online communities, and have conversations and connections with other people practicing alone (my online Magic Without Bullshit and Tarot Without Bullshit courses provide just such a space – and I love it)!

Do I Need A Coven?

No. You don't!

Also, if you do find a group of folks you want to practice with, it's not mandatory to refer to yourselves as a coven, contrary to what you may read on the internet.

Somehow, the word 'coven' has never felt quite right to me – but if you love it, use it! If it doesn't quite fit you and you'd really love to work with a group, there are so many other words you can use – group, circle, collective, and more.

You don't need to practice with a group of other witchy folks in order to be valid in what you do and in what you believe. In reality, it might be very, very hard to even find folks who believe the exact same things you do, and who want to practice witchy things in a way that feels compatible with your own worldview. It can be really fun coming together in a group, though – even if you find that you don't fully agree with each other on everything spiritually or magically, it can be exciting to explore and take turns leading ritual.

That being said, many will ask that you forget everything you think you know about your own beliefs and about magic in order to conform to their own particular ways of doing things. This was the case for every coven I spent time in, and while I am thankful for the opportunity to moonlight in a variety of spaces, ultimately, it wasn't right for me to submit to someone else's leadership. I decided it felt best to affirm my own sovereignty, experience, and connection to my magic and my spirits. You may feel the same.

Or, you may feel like you would love the structure of a coven or other regimented group of magical folks. If that's the case, great! The internet is a fantastic way to find local groups, if practicing in person is on your wavelength.

However, if you'd like some group connection, conversation, and mutual support outside of a typical 'coven' structure, and prefer to connect online, I've incorporated an online community and virtual live group coaching component to my online courses on both tarot and magic (Tarot Without Bullshit, and Magic Wiithout Bullshit, respectively).

Why? Well, I don't believe that coven-oriented practice is the only way to bond over magic with other people – and, sometimes, it really helps learners and newer practitioners to actually chat with others about how their energy work practice is evolving, ask questions of one another, and troubleshoot what exactly is going wrong when a spell or ritual you've done hasn't gotten you the results you were hoping for. I do know that sometimes practicing magic alone can feel like groping around hopelessly in the dark – which is why I include community as a crucial aspect of my online programs.

There's so many different ways to connect with other people – it doesn't all have to be in a 'coven' environment.

Should I Start or Join a Coven?

It's up to you! What I can tell you is, every group experience I've had in joining up or attending the covens of others, be they short term or long term, with friends or relative strangers… none of these experiences brought me what I wanted, which was community. A loving, kind community, that would challenge me and hold me in whatever I was going through. What a dream!

It's a lofty goal, and definitely something that many of us want to feel at some point: loved, accepted, held, cared or unconditionally.

In my experience and observation of myself and others in the last 20 years of being involved in witchcraft, sometimes the desperate desire for belonging can cloud our judgement and vision, can cause us to settle for something that doesn't feel right to us, with people whose beliefs or behaviours we don't agree with or don't like.

In my practice, I've rarely had any of my spell work just flat out flop. But, I have to say, my most memorable and straightforward magical failure was a working I did to summon magical community. I wanted to find a coven, a group of people who believed in magic and spirits, who felt energy, who could practice with me, hold space with me, work with me, as collaborators celebrating full moons or new moons or solstices or equinoxes or just the big bad beauty of life itself. I put all of my wishes into this candle, and every time I lit it, it would snuff itself out – windows closed, no wind anywhere in sight. This happened again, and again, and again, until the candle couldn't even hold its flame for more than a few minutes. In my decades of practice, I've never seen anything like it, before or since.

What was this candle's message for me? Was the universe flat-out denying my request?

Well, yeah!

At least, that's my interpretation of it.

Now that it's been years since this happened, I've been able to find some peace in shifting my perspective.

At first I was upset – disappointed and dejected. What's wrong with wanting a little community? Over time, I came to realize that I wanted community for something I would have benefitted from cultivating in myself – self-acceptance, self-love, a deeper dedication to magic, and a fierce trust in my own practice, without needing or wanting anyone else to validate me or tell me I was or am good and legitimate. When we're solely looking for external validation, we're moving towards a world of hurt. And I've been there!

Once I boosted up that internal validation – having strong faith in myself, my spirits, my spiritual experiences, I stopped seeking out communities that already existed, and started sharing more openly about who I am, what I practice and why, what I believe and why, and have found myself in a somewhat accidental position of what some might call community leadership. Create what you want to see in the world, right?

I don't have a coven – and I don't want one, other than my group of saints, spirits, and other beings I regularly work with – but I have stepped into witchy community in a different way by running online courses, group mentorship programs, and taking on spiritual consultation clients for mentorship in tarot and magic.

My path won't work for everyone, but it's how I've had to navigate this funny thing called 'community' – and yes, for me, an introvert, this is largely online! I do love public events and light right up at conferences, parties, and crowds, but I need my down time and feel most spiritually rested when I'm doing slow burn quiet magic in my apartment over time.

So, ok, ok, enough about me – how about you? Should you join a coven, or make your own coven?

This is such a deeply personal decision, and will boil down to so many factors.

First of all, I just want to underscore that not being in a coven or magical group where you practice together doesn't make you any less valid of a magical practitioner. Got it? Good! Don't get me wrong, community is great for so many things, but if we live our lives waiting and hoping for everyone to like and accept us before we accept ourselves, that seems like a total waste of time.

Some important questions to ask yourself might be the following:

- Why are you seeking a magical group? What do you hope to get out of it? What, realistically, do you have the capacity to give?
- How comfortable are you with leadership? No, really – I seriously underestimated the importance of this question in the early days of my public personhood in the witchy space. Now, it's something I think about and reflect on every day: What does responsible leadership mean to me?
- Do you want to be a leader, or do you want to follow a leader? Or would you like to find an egalitarian, non-hierarchial group where everyone shares leadership responsibilities? This last bit is often easier said than done.
- Do you actually like spending time with other people, or do you do better alone? Reflection question: do you secretly love when people cancel plans?
- Are you introverted or extroverted – and how does that play out in what you're looking for in your magical group happenings? Are you looking for a quieter group, or would you prefer one with a party hardy mantra that ain't afraid to get a bit wild?
- How aware/willing are you to shape healthy group dynamics? How would you deal with group dysfunction?
- What do you believe – and are you looking for a group where everyone believes more or less the same thing as you and works with the same divinities, or would you prefer a more eclectic, open group, with different members taking turns leading rituals from their own personal practices?
- How will you deal with differences in skill, belief, and personality in the group? How will you deal with different group members perhaps having different expectations about what the group is or can do for them?

Managing a group is a lot of work! Collaborative community projects and initiatives like covens, even when started with easy breezy intentions, can sometimes be exhausting and result in burn-out, especially when all the wrangling falls to one person. Think about being back in school, when you were assigned to do group projects. Who were you in that group?

It may sound like I'm coming across as very anti-coven – I'm not! Go in to the endeavour not just starry eyed, but with eyes open as to both how much work it can be, and also some potential road blocks or difficulties that might emerge, because it is, ultimately, like a spiritual group project – and whether you like it or not, anywhere there's people, there's conflict, despite the positivity and purity of our intentions.

ONLINE COMMUNITY

I was a weird androgynous kid in suburban Colorado. I didn't fit in. I read books on witchcraft (at home, in secret) when everyone else I knew went to church. I was androgynous at a time when that wasn't considered to be in any way okay. I was a socially awkward, kinda-goth. Needless to say, I found community online.

I did have some great friends in person as a kid, despite my awkwardness, but my real lifeline was the good ol' interwebs. I found my way into online message boards around fanfiction, art, web design, and, of course, all things animism, witchcraft, tarot, and magic. I participated in lots of online message boards and groups, most of which were likely not aware I was a teen. The internet was new, so we all went by false names, and no one exchanged photos – we all just learned together, at once wildly anonymous, on the other, incredibly intimate and raw. I'm super thankful for these old message boards – there was, of course, the occasional drama, but compared to today's internet, it's not even worth acknowledging. Everyone was generally pretty honest, chill, respectful, helpful, and curious. Conflict was dealt with in a generally diplomatic and egalitarian way. Moderation was a known and encouraged thing.

I've not found anything like that, in terms of online magical community, before or since – other than the environment I've cultivated in my Magic Without Bullshit and Tarot Without Bullshit online courses. I created these courses to be what I always wanted, but could never find – and I consider myself to be incredibly blessed that my courses are populated by so many sincere, brilliant, thoughtful, earnest, talented, and interesting, compassionate people. The entire internet may sometimes seem like a cesspool from hell where it's impossible to form genuine connections amidst the vitriol and outrage, but trust me – there are some lovely gems out there, looking for genuine connection and conversation.

Online community can help us connect with like-minded folks across time and space – which can be amazing if you, like my childhood self, live somewhere where you're the only one who believes what you believe. The internet can provide a space to explore new spiritual identities in a safe way, whether anonymous or named. You can share as much as you want, as little as you want – either in a public social media space like Twitter, Instagram, or Facebook, or somewhere closed and members only. And, in times where physical gatherings aren't desirable or accessible, online community can be a godsend – whether it's via email threads, message boards, social media, or endless Zoom calls.

chapter Seven

Ritual

WHAT IS RITUAL?

There will are as many definitions of 'ritual' in the magical and spiritual context as there are people who consider themselves to be practitioners of magic. There have been many books written about the semantics of what constitutes 'ritual' specifically, as opposed to just some mundane everyday task.

Ritual can involve repetition, a personal sense of specialness or sacredness, clusters of specific movements and rhythms, a constantly visited place where the ritual occurs; sometimes rituals ask of us to wear special clothing, to behave differently than we otherwise might. Rituals can involve rules and structure; they can be fluid, open, intuitive. Ritual can be formal, and it can be casual. Ritual can be something we do completely alone, in communion with our spirits, or it can happen in communities, where kinship is strengthened due to group participation in and knowledge of ritual.

Ritual can involve feelings of performance, decorum, and strength – as well as experiences of vulnerability, intimacy, and quietude.

Ritual is what you make it – what you open to – what you want from it.

Some of us may only wish to participate in group ritual – and to my introvert heart, that sounds absolutely terrible! My most potent magic happens alone.

We can work with(in) ritual to make magic, to do witchcraft – to transform our lives, to meet ourselves: maybe again, and maybe for the first time.

Ritual, no matter its form, is an invitation to acknowledge our intention – or, for some of us, to find it in the first place, as it sometimes takes some wrestling and unraveling in order to locate it. Ritual is an affirmation of our connection to ourselves, our spirit, the world around us, the plants, animals, rocks, skyscrapers, streets, microbes, air, sun – everything. Ritual is an affirmation that we matter. We are important. Ritual is a reminder to share our voice, if only for ourselves, if only for the beings with whom we share space; perhaps with family, with a partner, with friends, with our home, with our environment.

Ritual is a reminder that we have been here before, that we have so much further we can go, if we wish to; ritual is a reminder to notice how vibrant and alive our present always already is.

Ritual can be elaborate or simple; it can involve five bouquets of flowers, twenty statues, and an elaborately cooked meal – or it can be just you, sitting alone on the lakeshore, gazing up at the moon with a bag of candy.

Ritual is what you make it – and however fancy or chilled out, ritual can absolutely change your life, your magic, your relationship to spirituality ant to yourself.

MUNDANE ACTIVITIES

Ritual doesn't only occur in special, closed-off 'magic rooms' and anointed fancy robes that you're not too sure where to buy (or where you'd even wear them; let's be real).

We engage in ritual (and many of them!) every day of our lives – we often just don't think about our daily practices under the framework of 'ritual.' I assume you brush your teeth every day, take showers, eat food, drink water. Lately I've been living in sweatpants, but maybe you prefer to choose a fun outfit and shoes, put on some jewelry, a watch, or some fragrance to spice up your vibe and heighten your energy. Maybe you do this completely for yourself, with no regard as to whether anyone sees you all dressed up. Maybe you have rituals around skincare or makeup at the beginning and end of each day, or very specific routines each morning and evening, without which you feel out of sorts or just somehow wrong. (Anyone else feel completely unhinged without a coffee first thing?)

Ritual can be grounding.

It can be repetitive, connect us more deeply to time and place, to ourselves.

We may remember who we were the last time we did a particular ritual as a way of marking time. Maybe these are rituals around winter holidays and ushering in the new year, or the enthusiastic celebration of summer. I love looking back at my year ahead tarot readings annually, on New Year's Day – having that yearly ritual with myself, and rereading my journal entries and list of everything I've achieved and learned has really revealed to me my own internal and external shifts in ways I'm not sure anything else could.

If you examine the ebbs and flows of your life, I think you'll find rituals and routines everywhere you look.

These can be very personal rituals! They don't have to be rituals anyone else participates in or has even heard of or seen. Rituals don't have to involve candles, or night time, the moon, or even solemnness, prayer, and religiosity.

Ritual can be joyful, exuberant, casual.

Ritual can be silent; it can be loud.

Ritual can be sitting down to paint or create music, or to journal or work on your next novel.

Ritual can be a slow, steady beach walk once a week.

Ritual can be that bouquet of flowers you buy yourself every month, just because.

With a little intention, rituals like cooking food, cleaning your home, cleansing your body, and getting dressed can be infused with some incredibly potent magic.

Magic isn't always about what you do – it's also about how you do it, why you do it, and how you feel about it. Magic is about intention.

EVERYDAY MAGIC

Magic is the collaboration of many wills in order to create shift in accordance with that will.

I say 'many wills' even if you are a solitary practitioner, because even your candles, tarot cards, incense, offerings, ancestors, divinities, whatever it is, wills' are contributing to your magic, if you invite them into magic-making with you.

But/and, we make magic every day – even if we don't have a daily altar practice, or a daily habit of checking in with our spiritual team, or engaging in prayer.

I don't say this to undermine the beauty and specificity of magic.

Instead, I'd like to draw attention to the way we are creating ourselves and our lives every day.

We are all always already manifesting – some of us ineffectively, some of us with exacting precision, and perhaps most of us somewhere in between.

Every movement we make is a reflection of our thoughts, our feelings – how much or how little we're aware of ourselves, our wounds; what's unhealed in us; what our skills and joys and dreams are.

Do we move towards those dreams – and if so, how?

There is magic, of course, in that movement. To create what we want, to fall upwards, we must know where it is we'd like to go, and, preferably, also why.

We move in alignment with our thoughts, intentions, and feelings all the time. For some of us, our intentions may be upward facing, forward facing – some of us may be in a bit of a rut. I've been in either place, and I know each is its own kind of hard, its own kind of struggle. Each path is also its own kind of easy.

Engaging intentionally with magic, witchcraft, and spirituality involves a reclaiming of the truth that we are always creating our present, our future; we are always framing our past, whether it be actively or passively. We can choose to take some ownership over our journey, or we can choose not to. It's up to us!

I love that magic and witchcraft can help us remember our own agency: magic can lead us back to self-trust, to self-love, to self-care; to connecting with who we are, who we would like to pull forth from our bones into the present day from the stars and the earth.

Magic and ritual – whether it be everyday and mundane, or elaborate and explicitly mystical, can be a part of that alchemy, if we choose it.

HIGH MAGIC, LOW MAGIC

In terms of form and structure, I find it most effective to describe the different types of magic through the heuristics 'high magic' and 'low magic.' Of course, magic is fluid! Life is fluid, we are all fluid – and I don't share this breakdown here in order to promote rigidity, but rather to break down what magic is and can be in such a way that you might recognize yourself and your natural inwclinations in some of these descriptions.

Magic is such an enormous topic, and I realize it can be so incredibly overwhelming to start – so, at least with some of this introduction of the forms and 'shapes' of magic, you'll have some more tools and terminology to describe and research the type(s) of magic that feel most aligned to your heart and soul. If neither of these descriptors resonate, feel free to play – take what resonates, put it in your toolkit, and leave the rest here with love. And you don't need my permission to be creative, intuitive, and innovative in exploring what magic might look like and feel like for you.

As a quick note – I didn't come up with the terms 'high magic' and 'low magic' – and, as I'm sure you'll notice, there's definitely particular biases these phrases come loaded with, as a result of the context(s) in which they came into being. While you may read the words 'high' and 'low' and immediately think that one must be better than the other, this couldn't be further from the truth! Neither is superior or more official or more effective – they're simply different magical strokes for different magical folks.

These dichotomies are heuristics – that is, they're phrases often used in community that, while not perfect by any means, are good enough to have a conversation wherein everyone understands what's being spoken of. Heuristics are useful placeholders that enable us to better communicate; they're 'good enough for now' words and phrases. I'm not the biggest fan of binaries, and of course the high/low magic dichotomy is a bit of a binary. Please join me in imagining and embracing the many shades of gray between these poles of thought.

I don't share these categories for you (or me) to make them into cages.

The high and low do sometimes overlap. Depending on who you ask, they might even overlap quite often. After all, magical practitioners are innovative folks – we tend to love experimenting, being creative, and trying new things. That's how these forms of magic got here in the first place, after all!

If the words 'high' and 'low' taste bad to you when applied to magic, select new ones.

Maybe ceremonial magic and folk magic feel better to you. Maybe it's grimoire magic and magic from the heart, or the land, that resonates.

These categories are as beautiful as what we make them mean to us – not to constrain, or to help us constrain ourselves in ways that are not useful, but instead expansive. I share these categories – limited as they are – to be challenged, to be interrogated; to inspire you; to nudge a magical vocabulary further into bloom.

Sometimes, constraint can help us expand – either literally, into ourselves; like a butterfly after time in a cocoon.

Take what's yours, leave the rest – whether you find yourself high, low, or dancing somewhere along the midline.

LOW MAGIC

'Low' magic is the magic of the masses.

Low magic is intuitive. It is the feral cry of an animal, or you. It is following your inspiration to ecstatic dance and loudly stomp your feet at two in the morning, after even your cats have fallen asleep; it is the instinctual utterance of poems, of prayers, of wishes, hopes, dreams, desires, and even instructions to the universe, to your spirit team, to yourself.

Low magic can come from books, but doesn't always.

Low magic doesn't ask for permission, doesn't need it.

Rules, what's that? Never heard of them.

Low magic is folk magic. Low magic comes from the heart.

Low magic is magic you're always already doing, without always really knowing why or how.

Low magic can come from desperation, from need.

Low magic is healing.

Low magic is revenge.

Low magic is protection.

Low magic is the earth.

Low magic is the soil, and what and who bubbles up from beneath – the sounds and shapes of the oppressed fighting for themselves and each other, against any and all powers that be (and be, and be).

Low magic comes from below; low magic rises up.

Low magic comes from listening to yourself, to spirits, to your soul, to the souls of the earth; low magic is your ear on the sand, listening; low magic is speaking to the trees, low magic is kissing the earth, low magic is soil and earth and water and dirt, and you are the seed. Low magic is the fertilizer.

Low magic is trance, mediumship, possession; low magic is kitchen witchery, planting gardens, watching leaves grow, harvesting them, creating with them.

Low magic is divination on lopsided wooden tables, or maybe even just the grass.

Low magic is the sound of an inhale, an exhale.

It's here, it's felt, and then it's gone.

INTUITION AND INSTINCT

Low magic is all about following your intuition and your instinct.

This isn't to say that there's no place for fancy book learnin' in low magic – after all, I consider low magic my home, and as of this writing I'm halfway through a PhD and have a sizeable book collection which looks at magic from both academic and practitioner-based lenses.

Following our intuition doesn't mean we ignore everything we've read, or that we disrespect academia, research, history, and science due to some sort of ill-advised and romanticized anti-intellectualism.

Low magic just means that we listen to our core being as our primary anchor for what feels right – what to do, and when. Low magic, too, is rigorous – but in a wild, unbridled, self-knowing way.

Low magic makes a lot of room to listen to our bodies. How we feel, why we feel it; and we learn to feel out these topographies as inspirations for our movements as practitioners of magic.

In low magic, we honour our feelings, our intuitions, our instincts – not just in a lip service way. We scaffold our magical practice on top of it, with joy and trust and care, and in so doing we know that the universe will hold us, that our spirits and divinities will carry us forth into exactly where and who we need to be. Intuition is a map, our feelings topographic valleys and crests.

One thing I hear quite often from new magic learners is they're often afraid of following their instincts.

My email inbox is full of questions like, "Am I doing it wrong? Will I explode if I do a spell or ritual at the wrong time?"

I totally understand these fears and concerns, especially if magic is a newer practice – there's so much to learn, and as someone who has been practicing and living and breathing witchcraft for more than twenty years, I can tell you confidently that there's always more to learn!

Chances are, no, you won't explode! So don't worry!

I'm not someone who is a total relativist; I don't necessarily feel as though anything goes – there are certain practices that will help and hinder you, as discussed in a previous chapter on energy work – part of the fun and beauty of 'low magic' is feeling empowered to try things out and create your own rules, structures, and systems – even if you've never read anything even remotely similar in a book before, even if your 'system' is just going with the flow and moving intuitively with no particular rhyme or reason.

Low magic creates space for us to lean into our intuitions and instincts, to move around and explore, and to see where we land. Low magic honours instinct as a critical form of magic, and embraces fluidity and experimentation.

Stepping into Sponteneity

Within low magic, there's a lot of room for spontaneity, change, shift, and impulse. Not quite the full moon? No problem! What planetary hour is it? Does the practitioner of low magic care? Maybe, maybe not! (I don't!)

Those who resonate with this style of magic tend to thrive when they follow their feelings. Instead of planning rituals in exacting and elaborate to-be-followed-to-the-letter detail, these witches feel best when they respond to an urgent need, feeling, or inspiration for magic. Instead of being scared of or overwhelmed by following instincts and intuition, practitioners of low magic can thrive and feel most connected and creative in this space. It's definitely not a prerequisite for practitioners of low magic to be unyieldingly spontaneous, though I do find it is quite often the case!

So, if you're not the most spontaneous person but everything else about low magic resonates, sit tight. As there are gradations of order and organization, so too are there gradients of spontaneity. If you find joy in inspiration – and following it – that counts. Why not follow your joy, see where it leads you?

What I think many witches forget is that none of this started written down – it started with people feeling out the vibes of the universe, the spirits, the earth, the divine, and more – trying things out, and seeing what worked.

Chaos and Impulse

Low magic is also a place for chaos, for impulse. If you're like me this fills you with lightness and joy, and... if you're not, it might fill you with terror! I thrive by riding the chaotic and sometimes wild energy of the spirits I work with and the magic I do.

Since my style of working does tend to be spontaneous and intuitive, it probably comes as little surprise that this can sometimes mean rituals and spirit interactions that are a bit more chaotic than calm! Following intuition can mean riding the waves of energy as we feel them, and sometimes we find ourselves somewhere quite lively and surprising in our magical practice, our ritual, and our spellwork.

Chaos isn't necessarily a bad thing. If you're a person of extremes, like me, perhaps you'll enjoy periods of high intensity followed by long periods of rest. I like for my magic to echo this pattern, too – impulsive, chaotic energy can sometimes lead us to quite a special place, if we know how to steer our magical ship.

However, impulsive movement can also result in peace and stillness – it depends on what waves of energy you're noticing, feeling, and riding during that day, night, or season. If I have any advice, it's to be open to the myriad of shapes your magical impulsivities might take, whether they lead you into the outskirts of a storm, or in its calm centre.

HIGH MAGIC

What's often referred to as 'high' magic involves more ceremony, books, grimoires, ancient (or not-so-ancient) texts, graphs, tables, charts, symbols, glyphs, and inarguable correspondences. This magic has been historically practiced more often by so-called 'men of letters,' and so this form of magic is often called learned magic or ceremonial magic.

Of course all magic involves forms of learning and ceremony, but 'high' magic is often more about following rules or instructions set out in particular texts, many of which may seem quite obscure or esoteric to the average reader.

I have no complaint about high magic – after all, a little ritual, ceremony, and book learning never hurt anybody! However, it's certainly not my specialty, and it's not how I would describe my own practice, as much as I love reading old books and grimoires.

The workings of western esoteric orders such as The Hermetic Order of the Golden Dawn, Thelema, A∴A, the Qabalah, Enochian magic, Goetic magic, all fall under what I would refer to as high magic or ceremonial magic. Though much of the inspiration for this form of magic – and many foundational texts – can be traced to the sixteenth century and medieval and renaissance forms of magic, the nineteenth century revival of this philosophy of magical working enjoyed a resurgence in the nineteenth century, with such familiar names as Eliphas Levi, and later A.E. Waite and Aleister Crowley.

If you're someone who loves pomp, circumstance, grandiosity, order, planning, and following instructions, the occasional usage of ancient languages, you might find yourself drawn to this type of practice.

PLANNING AND ORDER

This form of magic often relies quite extensively on correspondences, planning, order, and structure – with glyphs, seals, charts, graphs, sigils, and diagrams. Within this framework, there tend to be more 'right' and 'wrong' ways to do things, and times to do them. Many grimoiric texts are quite explicit and uncompromising in their lists of correspondences – this spirit is like this, that spirit is like that, here is the symbol for each, you may only call them on this day at this time. (Some books even add in an 'or else!' here!)

High magic is highly organized, specific, and exact – and if you're someone whose being thrives with systems and structures, you might really resonate with how specific, detail-oriented, and 'extra' much high magic and ceremonial magic can be.

Organized Magic

Whereas low magic tends to be a bit more fluid and spontaneous, from my experience, high magic tends to be much more highly organized.

Practitioners of this style of magic do tend to lend quite a great deal of credence to correspondences, and charts and graphs of planetary numbers and planetary hours.

I dislike organization in my magical life as well as my mundane life (though they truly are the same!), and so while I'm always excited to attend workshops led by ceremonial magicians, this form of practice is not for me.

If you're someone who loves numbers, symbolism, patterns, and structure, this form of magic may resonate. This form of magic is less fluid, intuitive, and unplanned – rather, much is planned, thought-out ahead of time, without much wiggle room.

Of course, teachers and practitioners of ceremonial and high magic will also vary widely – so there is of course a spectrum on quite how exacting you need to be in order for ceremonial magicians to welcome you as one of their own.

The form of organization you see in high magic is generally quite a few orders of magnitude more intense than what you'll read about in this book – and, of course, it's possible to be a very organized practitioner of low magic, too! But, while related, I find the heart, energy, and structure of each practice – its motivations, framings, and overall vibe, are incredibly different.

chapter eight
magical timing

magical timing

MAGICAL TIMING

Magical timing is a topic that generally, folks either completely love or are incredibly stressed out by.

Perhaps in contrast to other spiritual and witchy writers, I don't see human standards of time as the only – or even preferable – way(s) to apprehend time. My relationship to time – due to my embodiment, my gender, and many other factors – will be different than yours, will be different from my aloe plant, will be different from the willow tree, will be different from the mountain, will be different from the ocean, from the coffee cup in my recycling bin, from my incense stick. It's typical for us as humans to impose our standards of understanding and categorizing time on all other beings, whatever their form – spiritual, plant, object, environment.

In some books you'll find long lists of timing correspondences – do this at that exact time, or else! And if that kind of thing resonates with you, awesome – there are tons of books that are a bit more alchemical, ceremonial, and exact in their charts and timings and mathematical calculations.

My approach to thinking about and feeling into timing is a little bit more fluid, and based more on my years of trial and error – as well as good ol' intuition. My aim here is to connect you to what feels right to and for you.

When's the right time to do something? Magic, prayer, ritual?

When it feels right.

When it feels aligned.

When the urge strikes you.

When you're in need.

I've done magic and ritual for each of those reasons – sometimes in the 'wrong' moon phase or the 'wrong' day of the week, according to most witchy manuals – and you know what? My magic still worked, felt powerful, changed me, changed my circumstances.

In this section, I explain how to relate to and feel into timing in a way that respects and acknowledges your own story and uniqueness – your own relationship to time. I'm less interested in giving you something to regurgitate and copy, more interested in leading you on a path back to yourself, where your own self-trust, self-knowledge, and intuition are sovereign.

LUNAR CYCLES

You can do rituals at any time, but with each moon phase you might wish to frame the ritual differently. Oftentimes folks get too hung-up on 'having' to do a ritual at a certain time. You can do a ritual at any time, as long as you're creative about your reasoning, phrasing, and intention.

Sometimes, we don't have the luxury of waiting until the next moon phase to do magic – sometimes we need to do magic immediately, especially if it's for the purpose of healing or moving through something visceral, intense, serious, or violent.

This list of correspondences moves from the waxing moon – when the moon moves from new/dark to beginning to grow and get larger, to full and bright and big, to getting smaller before moving into darkness once again. The correspondences and associations I list here are inspired by these movements – growing, shedding, vibrant fullness, and darkness.

WAXING MOON

Magic around this time is usually done to bring things to us or to create increase. If you were to do a ritual for healing during the waxing moon, you could envision the ritual as drawing and attracting healing into to your group and increasing the healing energies in your lives.

FULL MOON

Be careful - these energies pack a big punch! The full moon adds extra oomph to any magic done at this time. If you decide to do this ritual on a full moon, you can frame it in almost any way you want; with a full moon, you can't go wrong unless you're not very specific about what you're trying to achieve. If you want something a little more broad and generic about healing and transformation, this is a great time to work with that intent. Just know that you're welcoming in something huge with this lunar phase.

WANING MOON

This is a time to push things away from us – illness, bad habits, debt, etc. If you were to do a healing ritual at this time, you could frame it so that you banish any impediments to successful healing, and cast away any sickness and blockages to healing. If you wish to keep someone away from you, this is also a great time to ask for this type of manifestation.

New Moon

For me, this is a time for rest, introspection, refresh, and renewal. Strengthening opportunities and resolve to engage in self-care and creating healthy spaces to incubate and facilitate healing would be good uses of the energies associated with this moon phase.

Solar Cycles

Though the solar cycle is often ignored in favour of the supposedly 'witchier' lunar cycles, movements of the sun can be deeply potent ways to boost and bolster our magic. And, one benefit of connecting with solar cycles is that they happen daily, as opposed to the monthly cycle of the moon. So, if you need to do a ritual immediately, and can't wait for a particular moon phase – and/or don't want to frame your working in alignment with the moon phase you're currently in – working with solar energy is a great choice.

I think you'll find, too, that moving with an awareness of solar cycles will also shift how you relate to the flow of your day – no matter how explicitly magical, or subtly mundane. While the sun and the moon each give us a framework to think about and relate to temporality, do make sure to take the time to notice the differences in the energies of each being – the sun is not the moon, though they are both luminary bodies, powerful movers and shakers in the astral realm.

This correspondence list moves with a similar logic to that of the moon, and I hope the symbolisms will be quite intuitive! As we rise we grow and move into fullness with the light of the sun, and as the sun sets we shift into release and the stillness of the night. Depending on where in the world you live, each of these cycles may look quite different – you might experience long long days, long long nights, or some semblance of both.

Sunrise

As the sun begins to rise, magic that calls things to us is well suited. Also, any workings around new beginnings, fresh starts, planting seeds, ramping up, or drawing something to you. The moon phase equivalent of sunrise is the waxing moon.

High Noon

Whether it's at 12:00 noon on the dot, this solar time is when the sun is at its peak in the sky, its highest and hottest. Where you are in the world, this might not be at exactly that time, and it'll change as the seasons roll through your region. Regardless, high noon is the hottest part of the day, when the sun is exalted. We can link this time, high noon, to the full moon. As with the full moon, high noon is a jam-packed, powerful and potent time. This is a good time to do magic concerned with strengthening and amplifying a clear intention or goal.

SUN SET

As the sun falls, we see twilight. Darkness begins to make itself known, with a subtle hello, but hasn't yet completely conquered the land. Sunset is a great time for release, letting go, banishing, cleansing – getting rid of things and pushing them away from you. This solar cycle corresponds with the waning moon.

SUNDOWN

Otherwise known as night time: peace, reset, renewal. This station of the sun can be linked to the new or dark moon – a time of stillness, retreat, quietude, healing, and rejuvenation.

DAILY CYCLES

While we all have access to relationships with the sun as a way of connecting to and marking daily cycles, ultimately we will each have a different relationship to the cycles of each day. Maybe you work 9am-5pm, maybe you work night shift – or maybe you're a freelancer or entrepreneur whose daily schedule varies wildly based on what projects you have on and what clients you're working with. So, while I wake up around 10am every day, without an alarm, your morning rhythm may be different – maybe you get up at 4am every day to read, before heading to work at 6am. Maybe you get up to work out, to do art; maybe you do all that stuff after work instead. Maybe you don't have a typical job, and support family and children by being a stay-at-home parent, or maybe you're on social supports for unemployment or disability.

All of this is to say – another way to connect with magical timing is to notice the ebbs and flows and rhythms of your days. Do you love to start the day with coffee, and cuddle up in bed with a mug of tea?

Notice when you feel your best – when are you most energetic? Do you wake up bright-eyed and bushy-tailed, or do you take a few hours to become lucid, like me? Are you ready to pass out at 8pm, or are you a night owl?

Paying attention to – and moving with an awareness of – our own daily cycles and rhythms will only help boost our magic. How can you incorporate magic and ritual into the rhythms and flows of your day? Are there ways you already do that?

While it can feel mystical to notice the rhythms of celestial bodies like the sun and moon, I love attuning myself to my own daily rituals, rhythms, comings, and goings – and to create and set aside time for magic and prayer in a way that feels in flow with your daily movements.

Weekly Cycles

Maybe your 'weekends' are Tuesdays and Wednesdays. Maybe you're someone who doesn't even really know what a 'weekend' is – days off, what's that?! – and prefers to just spread your work or primary tasks across mornings (or evenings). Weekly cycles will look different for all of us, depending on the distribution of our time and energy, as well as the rhythms of our bodies and energy levels.

Is there a particular day(s) of the week where you feel particularly energetic or at peace? Have you designated any particular day as a self-care day, pizza night, date night, secret-dream-project day? Are there any days that feel most magical to you?

I considered listing some typically agreed-upon-in-Western magic correspondences for each day of the week. You know, that same stuff you'll find in every witchcraft 101 book – do magic for love on Fridays (a day often associated with love goddesses), money and prosperity magic on Thursdays (ruled by Jupiter, the planet of expansion), if you wanna fuck someone up do it on a Tuesday (ruled by Mars, god of war), and so on, and so on. I actually wrote a few of these out, then hit delete and took a breath.

If you want to learn of those correspondences – correspondences that other people have intuitively felt or decided by other means – there are many other books in which to do so.

But, truth be told – you may not give a shit about love goddesses, or Mars the god of war; you may not believe in divinities at all, and you might not care too much about mythology, Greek or Roman or Celtic or Buddhist or Hindu or otherwise.

I find that adhering to other peoples' rules about what the days of the week symbolize and mean, without cultivating an understanding of why or how we ended up with those linkages, magic learners can feel boxed in, confused, and scared to misstep or do something wrong. I'd rather my students cultivate a strong relationship with their own deep inner knowing around what the days of the week mean and symbolize to them and why – rather than simply go along with it because it's in a list in a book.

Feel free to look that stuff up! As always, question the list, throw it out and create your own; shift it, add to it, try it out and see how it feels. Over time, you'll notice how each day feels to you – and when you feel called to do different types of magic and ritual. To me, that's much more meaningful and spiritually significant, because it's based off of what resonates with you, your own personal 'why' – rather than simply the result of memorization of someone else's ideas and meaning making around time and dates.

MONTHLY CYCLES

I love working with monthly cycles! I'm a bit too intense and long-format not to feel rushed by the confines of a week; a month feels cozy.

One of my rituals around the new year is to pull cards for each month ahead – and to check in with myself as each month begins and end. How did the lessons of the tarot card of the month express itself? Did I rise to the occasion and learn, or did the month's happenings leave me feeling exhausted? Pulling one tarot card for each month helps ground my year. It helps me break the long expanse of time into manageable chunks, bite-sized enough to satisfy me without leaving me either hungry or too full.

This ritual keeps me connected to myself, my processes, and the greater picture – my goals for myself throughout the year, whether academic, spiritual, romantic, vocational, or otherwise.

Perhaps you have monthly cycles of your own.

Are these biological? If you menstruate, you may wish to incorporate these cycles of your body into your processes of magic. Maybe this holds absolutely no interest for you at all, even if you do – totally cool. Listen to your body and what feels good and right. Personally, I haven't menstruated in more than a decade – I am as of this writing on my third IUD, and it stops my periods! This is a gender-affirming choice for me, and has always felt right. I include this little bit of TMI because I believe representation is important – I've never read another witchy book that acknowledged the predominance of menstruation in the way gender and femininity are talked about in a lot of witchy spaces. If you're trans, your body might have different types of monthly cycles, like I do – which may be biological or not. Hell, you don't have to be trans for your body to have a mind of its own, and have its own logics and timings around what it does and doesn't do as time moves along. All of that doesn't make you less of a witch, less a practitioner of really powerful magic.

How do you mark each month, if you do? Maybe it's through your body, maybe it's through the moon, through astrological seasons – maybe it's with a monthly tarot pull or ritual, or something else entirely.

Or, maybe you resonate with a quarterly arrangement of time, since it matches your business' tax payment schedule. Perhaps semesters feel more natural to you, if you're a student or teacher, or have kids who are in school. All good! Notice what feels right, and work with it. Maybe none of that resonates with you. What does? I'm sure if you take a moment to think about it and reflect, you might notice some monthly cycles that recur in your life.

Notice these rhythms, whether internally imposed or externally imposed, and reflect on whether these monthly rituals support you.

Are there ways you might be able to incorporate more magic into your monthly cycles? Do these cycles and their movements already connect you to your magic?

Astrological Cycles

Astrological systems and frameworks break the year (or even years, plural) into different chunks of time, which may be ruled by different signs, characteristics, qualities, and attributes. If we wish to, we can work with how and what each chunk of time is 'ruled' by to best align our magic and our spiritual and mundane efforts.

You don't need to be an astrological expert to be a magical practitioner who does successful witchcraft. If you want to ignore astrology completely, you totally can! But there are ways – that don't involve reading one million astro-books – to move with an awareness of astrology within your magic. Don't fall into analysis paralysis – it's important to take some action, too!

For instance, I love to work with an awareness of Western astrology's twelve signs, and the energies they bring into each astrological season (or month, in other words) that they rule. Since Aries is the first sign of the Western zodiac, it's a powerful energy for starting something big with a bang – with the propulsion of any fire sign. Scorpio, for instance, is a sign of death, rebirth, and transformation – so, while Scorpio season tends to be rough for me, I can work with that transitional energy to intentionally embrace any shedding that needs to happen, however uncomfortable. Other witchy folks, depending on their astrological depth, may feel inspired to be a bit more specific in their magical alignment to the astro-world – and plan ritual around significant planetary events in the cosmos. I do do that sometimes myself, though I am more intuitive than anything. It's more common for me to intuitively do big rituals, and then find out later that some significant astro-event happened at exactly the same time.

There are so many different ways to incorporate the planets, the stars, and astrology in general into your magic – both in how you practice, and when you practice.

Though Western astrology is my main go-to frame of reference, I also move with a (very, very limited) awareness of Chinese and East Asian astrology. If you're from these regions, you may have grown up with this form of astrology, and so that may feel like a better framework for you and your magic.

For my first fifteen years in Toronto, I lived in Chinatown – with ten of those years right next door to a Chinese Buddhist temple. My landlord was Chinese, and we'd talk often about Chinese New Year as it came and went, and he would explain what each turn of the year meant for our sign (we are both Snakes).

Every year, I'd go next door to the temple, light some incense, donate some money, and pick up some fortunes and good luck charms for the new year. I found that cultivating an awareness of what the coming and going of each animal's year meant was incredibly meaningful, both personally and spiritually.

Maybe this form of astrology is what you resonate most with culturally – maybe you have Chinese or East Asian heritage, and this style of astrology is something that you grew up with and know like the back of your hand. In that case, you can write this section yourself, superstar! There's absolutely no reason you can't work with this incredible astrological knowledge to inform your own spiritual and magical practice, as you explore what witchcraft and magic mean to and for you.

There are many more forms of astrology than I've listed here – including Islamic astrology, Babylonian astrology, Vedic astrology (otherwise known as Hindu astrology or Jyotisha), Burmese astrology, Mayan astrology, and more. Just because Western astrology gets the most media play in witchy spaces, doesn't mean it's the only astrological approach worth considering.

Seasonal Cycles

I love seasonality. I'm not too sure I could ever move anywhere with no seasons – I think I might feel crazy, like time is standing still. Seasons help me mark, notice, and understand the passage of time in my own life – and in the environment that holds me. I see cycles of life and death reflected in the seasons where I live in Toronto – where we have distinct spring and fall seasons of in-between, and then extremes of hot and cold, with our summers sometimes reaching as hot as 40 degrees celcius, and our winters as cold as -40 celcius.

While this may sound extreme, I kinda love it. Before I bought clothing appropriate for each season, I wasn't a fan – but over the years I've learned to let each of Toronto's four seasons guide me through birth, growth, decline, death, and rebirth.

What do the seasons look like where you live? I don't want to create a list of correspondences based on the climate and seasons where I live – I know the world doesn't revolve around Toronto!

Maybe where you live, the seasons aren't separated into the quadrants of spring, summer, fall, and winter. Maybe where you live, you have two seasons – the rainy or wet season, and the dry season. Or, maybe your region marks seasonality based on environmental events. When I lived in Colorado, we definitely had tornado season – and I know other regions might have wildfire season, hurricane season, monsoon season. Some regions separate seasonality into six!

Unfortunately, I find a lot of conversation and teaching in witchy communities doesn't make space for how many different types of ways of organizing and understanding climatic and ecological shifts there are. If you live in Jakarta, Santa Fe, London, Stockholm, Mumbai – you'll have a completely different relationship to season, climate, weather, and seasonal shift than I do in Toronto.

How would you describe each season of where you live? How can you tell when it's arrived? Do you have any rituals or practices that honour the transition into each season? Do you associate each season with any particular series of rituals or practices, or areas of focus in your life – for example, cleansing, renewal, rebirth?

Embrace the special, unique seasonality and specificity of where you are! You don't have to be in any particular climate to be a witch or to practice witchcraft. Magic is everywhere.

Cycles of the Year

How you relate to the cycles of the year will differ depending on where you live, and your region's relationship to what marks seasonal shift. Some cultures and regions have spiritual or religious holidays that mark the cycle of the year – others may celebrate solstices and equinoxes. Where I live in Toronto, most folks I know do celebrate Christmas – even the non-Christians among us! Holidays may transcend their religious roots and become cultural celebrations.

How you relate to the cycles of the year will differ depending on where you live, and your region's relationship to what marks seasonal shift. Some cultures and regions have spiritual or religious holidays that mark the cycle of the year – others may celebrate solstices and equinoxes. Where I live in Toronto, most folks I know do celebrate Christmas – even the non-Christians among us! Holidays may transcend their religious roots and become cultural celebrations.

No religion has a monopoly on holidays that witches 'need' to practice in order to be witches – though I know it may often feel that way given the common community discourse! The popularity of contemporary western-style neopagan witchcraft grew out of Wicca, from the 1950s onwards and starting in England, spreading to the United States, Canada, Australia, New Zealand, and around the world. The typical 'witches' wheel of the year' is based on Wicca's interpretation of what they understood to be ancient pagan holidays of yore – and, unfortunately, it seems like a lot of the witchiverse has completely lost sight of these holidays, in the form that we know them today in popular witchy culture, originated in Wicca, and otherwise don't have too much to do with witchcraft writ large.

What holidays am I talking about? Well, the eight Wiccan holidays of Ostara, Beltane, Yule, Lughnasadh, Samhain, Imbolc, Litha, and Mabon – which you do see talked about as kinda pan-witchy holidays. I remember when I was ten years old and first dipping my toes into this whole 'witchcraft' thing, pretty much every book on witchcraft that I read talked about these holidays, or 'sabbats', as though they were mandatory – even the books that had nothing to do with Wicca!

In case it isn't abundantly clear, you don't have to have a particular relationship to the neopagan 'wheel of the year' to be a witch. You don't have to have any one way of relating to the changes of seasons, to holidays, to any of it. You can celebrate absolutely no holidays whatsoever. You can celebrate winter solstice, but not Yule or Christmas. You can also go hard on Christmas, and ignore the solstice. You can do December holidays – and any and every holiday, or lack thereof – on your own terms, without having to be bound by what anyone else is doing. Ostara isn't mandatory. None of it is mandatory.

Your relationship to the turning of the year is yours.
It's unique to you.
And that's awesome.

All too often, I see folks having a relationship of self-imposed (and, to be honest, seemingly community-imposed) feeling of obligation towards the celebration of holidays, events and rituals that can mark the turning of the wheel of the year.

One thing that always struck me is that the mythologies behind those 'witchy' holidays, as popularized by Wicca, never felt right to me. There was all this talk of 'The' God and 'The' Goddess, the oak and holly kings, something about the sacred marriage of the god and goddess, or something, aka... sex. None of this has ever been my thing – at all. (And hey, if it's yours – firstly, no judgement, and secondly, lucky you! Most books on Wicca and Wiccan inspired forms of witchery will resonate with you – and there are tons and tons of books that fit this description.)

I've lived in a big bustling city for the last sixteen years. While a lot of the generic neopagan holidays can be related to in symbolic ways even though they're based on agricultural cycles and ecological shifts... sometimes this really hasn't been enough for me.

So, instead, I've created my own seasonal markers and 'cycle of the year' of sorts! I'm still learning the rhythms of my new-to-me neighbourhood, and I noticed a distinct cycle and marking of shifts in time in my previous area, and created my own little seasonal markers that helped me notice yearly beats.

My old apartment was next door to a temple, and across the street from a skating rink, park, and pool. Spring started when I could hear the click-clack of skateboards on the patches of asphalt right outside my window. Summer was marked by the swimming pools opening, the end of summer by pools closing. Winter began when the skateboard rink was glossed over with smooth ice, skater kids replaced by families and couples skating circles in the ice. I'd hear chanting and bells from the temple next door, so the lunar new year also marked the yearly movements and cycles in my immediate environment.

What are the yearly rhythms for you? Which transitions, seasons, holidays, or other occasions do you feel called to notice, honour, celebrate? Maybe for you that's as simple as reveling in the seasons as they come and go, or honouring most (if not all) full or new moons. Maybe the 'new year' starts for you on Halloween, which some talk about as the 'witches new year' – but maybe it actually starts on the new calendar year for you, or the lunar new year, or even the spring equinox.

I know it may sound stressful or overwhelming to design your own wheel of the year – after all, many of us turn to books when we're looking for answers, explanation, and understanding. Having the burden of that investigation and knowledge thrown back on our shoulders isn't always fun.

But hat momentary discomfort is so, so worth it. Why? Because reflecting on your own seasons, cycles, rhythms – both within yourself and in your community and environment – will create a wheel of the year unique to you, and as such whatever rituals that are birthed or inspired from this work are more likely to be sustainable pillars of your spiritual practice. When we just follow instructions from someone else's wheel of the year, without thinking too much about if it actually aligns with our own belief system(s), cosmology, or values, it's a bit easier to fall off the 'wagon' – when something lacks meaning and personal significance, it can feel like a chore, and we can lose motivation to engage in our spirituality.

Some questions to ask yourself as you explore this are:

- What are your favourite times of the year? Least favourite?
- Are there any holidays, holy days, or celebrations that you really love and look forward to? These can be as varied as New Year's, your birthday, your favourite saint's holy day, the anniversary of a graduation or new job, anything! No day is too big or too small.
- How does your energy look throughout the year? Are you energetic in summer and tired in winter, or vice versa?
- Do you like big, formal, community rituals, or do you prefer when special moments are a bit more quiet and low key?
- Are there any times of year you feel obligated to celebrate? Does this align with you? Why or why not?
- If you could map out your ideal wheel of the year, that acknowledges everything that's important to you – how might it look?
- How does it feel good to you to understand and categorize the year? Perhaps you love the system of 12 months, or really see the year as two halves of a whole (wet season and dry season, dark part of the year and light part of the year, energetic half and slow half). Maybe you like a semester based timeline, as many teachers and students do – or perhaps the year makes most sense to you as quarters. How do these structures figure into your year? How does each phase feel distinct from the last?

chapter nine
magic in action
magic in action
action

SAMPLE SOLO RITUALS

Though I believe that all magical practitioners, witchy people, and folks interested in spirituality benefit from creating their own rituals, I realize it can be incredibly helpful for newer witches – or even just witches looking for some inspiration and fresh perspectives – to read and look over rituals and spell work created by others. Feel free to read these solo rituals as inspiration – or, you can copy them exactly, adapt them to yourself, your own circumstances, try them out!

Working magic alone is my favourite way to practice; I am perhaps shockingly a little bit of an introvert, and love doing magic that I can only do by myself: magic that focuses on me, healing my wounds, cleansing myself of what holds me back, planting and cultivating seeds that will help me be fully present, understand my past, and plan for my future.

As you read, it may be useful to make note of what resonates with you, what doesn't, and what inspires you to jump off from and change as a base for your own workings.

Do any of these sample solo rituals inspire you to create brand new rituals and spell-work that is just your own?

MORNING COFFEE ~~AS~~ AS RITUAL

More mornings than not, I take a short walk.

As an entrepreneur with no set schedule and an itinerary that can shift radically from one day to the next, these early morning (or sometimes afternoon) coffee walks can be a deeply stabilizing part of my day – sometimes the only common thread between days that otherwise always look quite different.

Recently, one of my students asked about my daily and weekly routines, and after some reflection I had to honestly answer that for the most part, I have absolutely no routine. No two days of mine look even remotely alike – and I like it this way! My efficacy shifts from day to day depending on what my body is doing, and as someone living with trauma and multiple disabilities it has been important for me to cultivate an attention and sensitivity to my radically fluctuating capacities. The best-laid plans – of course – aren't terribly reliable when living with the disabling effects of trauma.

Instead of judging my productivity, I've embraced a non-judgmental responsiveness towards my body.

Chatting with my student also inspired me to remember that I've always organized my time around deadlines. I like to focus on what's directly in front of me, hustle like crazy, rest, and move along to the next thing, one step at a time, one day at a time.

Having reasons to leave my apartment studio/office can be very helpful, and my morning coffee ritual serves this purpose – among others – for me. In a routine with no routine, this simple near-daily morning coffee ritual is a process of stabilizing, taking the time to check in with myself, with my insides and my outsides. Of being in my body and creating space for that body to intuitively lead me to wherever it wants – down this street, down that street. It's a practice in listening.

That's one thing I really enjoy about this little routine – it gets me in my body in ways that are pleasant and sensual rather than painful or uncomfortable.

The coffee I drink is hot and delicious and feels good in my mouth. I like feeling the warm liquid move through my insides, I like discerning the difference between flavours and textures at each espresso bar in my neighbourhood, noticing how each non-dairy milk brings out different flavours in the espresso. I like how it wakes me up, gets my ideas flowing, makes me excited to work.

Sometimes it can be difficult to feel motivated to get out of bed. Coffee wakes me up, invigorates me, makes me feel excited to begin fresh.

My little walks – depending on the shop I choose, and whether or not I'm in the mood or have the time to walk down to the water – take between 15 minutes to two hours. This is time just for me, to watch the world wake up, to be alone with my thoughts and check in with myself. To plan my day and see what I feel like working on, what I feel able to work on. Taking – and prioritizing – this intentional moment to pause and reconnect with my body, mind, and soul has become a really important part of my day, and something I'd rather not do without.

Would I save a lot of money if I didn't have a coffee everyday? Yeah, totally. Can everyone afford a coffee from a coffee shop every day? No. Does everyone want to spend this much money on coffee? Again, no. As someone who works in the same space I sleep, I see it as a more enjoyable alternative to spending that sweet coffee money on renting a shared office space.

This little morning ritual connects with me with my senses. With my body. My tongue, my stomach, my mind. This simple ritual connects me with my feelings. Leaving my apartment to go on a little walk is something I experience as an intentional reset, an intentional reconnection to myself. In a world where femininely gendered folks often have to un-learn a constant attention to other people at the expense of themselves and their own needs and interests, I see this act as a crucial one, of reclaiming space on my own terms, reclaiming ease and comfort.

One small step at a time. One little ritual at a time.

Maybe you hate coffee, or maybe you're just flat broke. Or both! No problem – there are still so many other ways you can engage intentionally to carve out little moments in your daily (or almost daily) lives in a ritualized way. There are so many ways to deeply ground and centre yourself, with or without spending anything at all.

Maybe you'd prefer to make coffee or tea at home and go on a little walk. I did this religiously in my undergrad – I'd brew herbal tea at home, take it with me in an enormous mason jar, and take it on a walk or just to class. At that time in my life I was seventeen and beyond broke, but I still wanted to go on walks with a comforting hot beverage. Whatever your financial constraints are, be creative!

Maybe walking isn't really your thing, and you'd rather sit in bed meditating every morning, first thing – or, every evening, right after you brush your teeth.

However we carve out this time and space to reconnect with ourselves, to be silent and still in our own bodies, to be attentive, to pay attention to and notice and listen our own (mis)alignment(s) – the doing of these rituals is so important. Each small and mundane ritual is part of a bigger picture, a cumulative relationship with ourselves, with our spirit and our environment.

I'm not saying everyone needs to start every day by going to grab a coffee from your local spot. But: my little ritual of doing this – a ritual that evolved pretty naturally, without much intention at all – has become a savored and holy part of my day. If I'm feeling unwell, it's a quick way to bring myself back on track. If I miss it, I don't feel quite right.

My attachment to this ritual has led me to spend some time reflecting on exactly why it is that this simple series of actions is so important to me, and why I will fight hard to keep being able to do it. For me the ritual is so much more than just buying a fancy oat milk flat white.

We all take time to treat ourselves in different ways – or, at least, I hope we do! If you don't, why not start now? Maybe that's something like getting your nails done once a month, or getting a haircut every two weeks. Maybe that's buying the fanciest beard oil that you can afford, or splurging on some cool locally produced cologne. Whatever it is, we all benefit when we have little rituals where we invest (be it time or money or both) in ourselves, in our well-being.

I'd like to invite you to take this full moon as an opportunity to take an inventory of what you do for yourself in a ritualized (that is: intentional, repeated, again) way.

How do you care for yourself? What are the little things you do regularly to make yourself whole again when you fall off the wagon? Maybe you do these after feeling depleted, or maybe you do them right before you hit that threshold. There are little rituals we put in place because we notice we feel good when we do them.

What are your little rituals?

Maybe we feel more like ourselves, more light and energetic, refreshed, calm. Maybe we just wanna honour that we really love the taste of a good donut, diets be damned! Some people start every morning with a smoothie or going to the gym – some of these rituals can feel untouchable, sacred, immovable. Sometimes it can throw us off to be thrown off our routines, or thrust away from our little rituals due to random circumstance. Pay attention to this! It's all crucial information about yourself: what feeds you, what depletes you, what stabilizes you.

Here are some questions for reflection. Feel free to journal about them, or even simply just turn them over in your mind. It's up to you!

- How do you replenish yourself?
- How do you connect to yourself?
- Do you take enough time to yourself, to connect with your flesh, body, mind; your senses?
- Do you take the time to check in with yourself to see how you're feeling?
- Do you take the time to be silent? To listen?
- What do you do to feed your body, mind and soul?
- What little pleasures in life do you look forward to?

These can be big, they can be small. They can be things you haven't told anyone about, that you never share. Or these rituals can involve big groups of people, be enormous communal events.

It's common to make the mistake of thinking that ritual needs to be big, long, loud, dramatic, with lots of bells and whistles and a special outfit. Nope. It can be as simple as the little pleasures we hold close to our hearts and cherish as the little rituals they are.

These actions and habits may help us to better access ourselves, in order to inspire a shift in mindset, body feeling, a shift in consciousness.

When done again and again, with intention:

These are the powerful stirrings of ritual.

Little by little.

THE MUNDANE MAGIC OF SELF-SOOTHING

It's three in the morning, and I can't sleep. Or, at least, it feels like three. Or maybe four? Hmm. I peek outside and can't decipher the exact shade of twilight. I make pretend like I'm asleep. I don't move. I breathe deeply. A five-o-clock alarm goes off. He gets up for a moment to feed the cat. Comes back to bed. Seems asleep, but perhaps is also pretending. We have a few hours left until the real alarm. First nights are always hard.

In this scene years ago, I'm recently single. I've been very happily leaning into this, spending time here and there with a handful of lovely souls who truly could not be more different from each other. As things escalate, I sometimes find myself in someone else's bed. Or, I find them in mine. These beginning moments in dating are often visceral in the way they force us to confront our relationship(s) with intimacy, proximity and closeness, and as someone with complex trauma, I find these times both deeply enjoyable and deeply challenging.

Dating is, of course, always ritualized.

Whether we're spending time with someone we've been seeing for ages, or if we're in a clumsy dance with someone new, there's always elements of ritual and repetition involved, mixed with splashes of surprise, curiosity, and novelty.

Some of this newness may be fun or exciting, and some may be scary.

I remember growing up with the awareness that my body being nervous about something was quite similar to what it did when it was excited; there was an importance here in awareness and reframing, and that continues for me today, still! A common characteristic of CPTSD is vigilance – constant, and often when it is no longer necessary.

This vigilance creates feelings of unsafety when there is no threat.

The body is agitated, nervous, anxious, nauseous, often with a racing mind. I hadn't eaten anything strange, didn't drink too much, but I felt like I was going to throw up, and like it would be dangerous to fully relax into the folds of an unfamiliar bed or body. I had been here in this feeling before, many times. Enough times to know that it wasn't the other person, it wasn't anything I ingested, it wasn't any actual unsafety – it was just my trauma making itself known; a familiar bodily ritual.

In a recent session with my therapist, we discussed one of my core wounds from childhood – the fear that if I was unwell or sick and communicated this to others, that those others would ignore what I said, and leave me to suffer alone, as a burden, rejected. To this day I feel completely comfortable alone at all times; I know I can take care of myself. Put me in a room with someone else overnight, and I suddenly panic and feel that if I should need help or care for any reason, I will not be cared for. So, in order to not lose my mind, I often need to self-soothe in these early days of dating, until I grow to trust someone, and my body relaxes without effort.

How is this relevant to ritual and witchcraft?

As magical practitioners, energy work is a crucial part of what we do, as is the ability to work with and harness energy in order to shift both our internal state and our external state.

Magic has often been defined as the art of changing consciousness at will.

So, what else, then, is my little self-soothing exercise but a form of magic, a little ritual – incredibly mundane though it may be? All spell work is done with the intention to create shift – to manifest a job, a partner, nice sex, easy money, protection, whatever it is.

And those are all a much bigger physical ask than simply creating a change inside our own bodies and minds.

Or is it?

Trauma creates biological difference. Traumatized people are simply wired differently from those without trauma in our histories, and changing our internal state at will can often feel incredibly difficult if not impossible. Therapies are often long-lasting and conducted over long periods of time in order to gain best results. So why not look to our magical skill set that we use in ritual in order to help shift our consciousness?

That's what I've been trying to do in these situations! It's not always easy and results aren't always immediate, but I've found that they do come.

So, what did I do?

Lying there, while pretending to be asleep so as to not arouse concern, I started to engage in similar practices that I might if I were beginning to slip into a ritual headspace.

First, I worked on grounding myself: breathing in and out in equal doses in order to calm down my nervous system.

Often, stabilizing the breath can be incredibly helpful in creating calmness. The type of breath I find useful here involves an equal count of time spent breathing in and breathing out, and in yoga is referred to as ujjayi breath. (When writing this, I decided to do a few minutes of research just to check – and it turns out there actually is some scientific research [as well as tons of anecdotal evidence, obviously] about this type of breath's impact on the nervous system, particularly around patients with trauma – basically, it releases tension, among other things!) This type of breath does sound like what you hear when you put a seashell to your ear when you do it properly, but it's possible to also be quite quiet – so I was!

With each breath out, I envisioned my anxiety (excess energy) trickling out of my body, through the house and into the earth beneath. With each inhale, I drew up calmness.

Throughout this breathing practice, I repeated a simple series of affirmations in my mind, based on what I thought the core fear or issue I had was.

This was something around fear of unsafety and abandonment, and so the affirmations I came up with were, "I am calm, I am safe, I am loved." Over time, my stomach ache went away, and once I was relaxed enough to not feel nauseous, the breathing and affirmations calmed me down enough – and grounded me – so that I could finally fall asleep and catch a few hours.

I also created a shield around myself and the entire room I was in. I did this by envisioning a giant white light sphere around myself, the bed, and the person I was with. Inside this shielded space I imagined all tension, fear, and anxiety trickling out, to be replaced with calmness and peace. It took a little while to solidify and for all of my agitation to dissipate, but it happened!

You might be thinking, Okay, Sabrina, what the hell – this is such a cop-out, I signed up here to learn about magic, not about how to chill out when you're anxious. But, I'd argue back – this is all part of the point.

When we relegate/delegate witchcraft and magic to only be about spooky or special things, things we delineate as mystical, it's easy to forget that basic energy practices can be helpful when applied to any other areas of our lives.

If magic involves changing consciousness at will, isn't the little series of practices I engaged in late that night a successful magical act? Isn't it immediately palpable witchcraft?

We are living in a time where it seems like either spiritual bypassing or acquiring material goods is how contemporary witchcraft is being sold in the mainstream. I'm all for buying new stuff – and having the money to do it – and I'm all for healing trauma and learning to feel 'well.' But the flashier moments of witchcraft – the big wham-pow of landing a new job or finding a good romantic partner – often eclipse the smaller, simpler moments like the one I'm sharing with you now.

This is a big part of how and why witchcraft matters.

We don't need to create a giant altar and buy fifty candles and put on our favourite spooky robe in order to be doing ritual; the only robe I ever do magic in is a bath robe.

So, should you choose to accept it, your ritual witchy homework is to reflect deeply on your own personal rituals of soothing.

Do you have a formula? Do you involve the breath?

What for you feels agitated the most: your mind, your physical body? Your emotions? What magical techniques might be appropriate in these moments? For me, since my physical body was indeed agitated, I wanted to use techniques that were also physical: intentional breath. My mind was going crazy with a bunch of thoughts, and so I replaced them with new thoughts: affirmations.

In magic it's common to state what we desire – bluntly – and so this is the principle of spell working I used in this case.

Grounding and shielding are also crucial energetic and spiritual techniques that I use in ritual all the time.

When thinking of little ways of ritually soothing yourself, think of how you approach ritual itself in your own magical practice.

Are you big on energy work? Shields, grounding, prayer, affirmation, cleansing? See what magic you're able to do without any of your objects or physical tools. One beautiful thing I love about witchcraft and magic is that once we learn these skills, and increase our proficiency with them, we'll be able to get results with our eyes closed, lying in bed next to someone, experiencing profound shift, with them none the wiser.

BUILDING A SELF-LOVE ALTAR

I fucking love pink. I know, I know, that's not very punk rock of me, but whatever! Whenever I create an altar for the specific purpose of honouring and loving myself, pink is the colour that tends to dominate the scene and feels natural for me as a visual embodiment of this energy.

The types of magic I do are informed by largely Western symbolisms and colour associations; red tends to dominate Western cultural visuals concerning love and romance. I associate the more subdued version of red – that is, pink – with platonic love, self-love, and friendship.

What matters in magic is that the colours you choose to work with have personal resonance for you personally, so that you are able to connect to the symbolic and literal power they have for you.

If associations and correspondences seem random and disconnected to your own personal associations, don't work with them! Much of your magic's potency may be lost if you do. Every element of magic and ritual should be intentional, and connected to what we feel deep in our bones.

Magic is most powerful when we can connect to each element of what we're doing and why: when we know why each herb is being used, when we know why each colour is being used, and when we know why we should use a candle of one shape instead of another.

Have you made an altar to honour your brilliance and your love for yourself? If not, why?

All too often, people perceived as women, femme, feminine, and/or gender non-conforming are called arrogant if we dare to have and show our self-love, self-worth, and self-respect. Our belief in ourselves is seen as a threat – how dare we be anything but timid and self-deprecating! How dare we prioritize ourselves!

If you can believe it, the individual I dated when I painted my graphic novel – in which I constantly depict myself – suggested I change my drawings of myself to be "uglier, so people can relate more." Somehow I still dated this person for an additional six months after this (!) – that's how ingrained these incredibly harmful and toxic narratives can be. We see them as normal, and often don't even react to it, just like I didn't when I was younger. Itt took me some time to actively retrain my brain.

It can feel totally overwhelming and scary to really step into ourselves, to dare to treat ourselves the way we would like others to treat us, to re-parent ourselves (if/when necessary), to soothe, comfort, and affirm our radiance – to affirm that we deserve love, care, appreciation, kindness, and good treatment. To appreciate the things we have accomplished, as well as the beauty of who we are, regardless of anyone else and aside from anyone else's (in)ability to see us as we are.

I know! It's scary to step into self-worth and self-love – because if we truly go there, go deep, it means we may be faced with the need to mourn all of that which we have robbed ourselves of in the past, perhaps due to fear of loss, or ignorance around any other option existing. The knowledge that we could have welcomed more into our lives earlier may be hard to face; I know it was for me.

Creating an altar to honour yourself may strike you as an icky idea, something that is too painful or uncomfortable, or maybe something you'd encourage your friends to do but that you'd never consider doing for yourself on your own behalf.

The idea of creating an altar for ourselves, by ourselves, about our love for ourselves may seem a bit tacky, arrogant, self-important.

It isn't.

You are worth celebrating, just as you are.

If we wait for others to celebrate us, we may be waiting a long time – and our value must come from inside, we must know it in our hearts rather than waiting for and being tied to any extrinsic affirmation for our mood and healthy self-concept. No. We do not need anyone else's permission to celebrate and honour our love for ourselves. It may feel weird at first, but I encourage you to push through those uncomfortable feelings. A lot of growth hides there, ready to be unleashed.

If our self concept isn't healthy – if we don't believe that we deserve to be treated with respect, if we don't believe at the core of our being that we deserve to be truly happy – it's unlikely that our magic will be truly successful in any meaningful and long term way.

Magic is fierce, it is regal, and its success comes with an embodied knowing that we can get what we wish to have if our relationship with the land, our spirits, and energetic collaborators (plants, animals, ancestors, and more) is strong and true and potent.

Often we are the ones holding ourselves back; a ritual and a spell is only as strong as the weakest link; love yourself to ensure that weakest link is not you.

So. How to do this on a practical level?

Begin by reflecting on what you love most about yourself. These can be external qualities, internal qualities, whatever – it can also be things that you have accomplished, experiences that you survived. I would encourage thinking through a balanced mixture of these different qualities. In alignment with Western magic, practices, a useful outline to think through this may be to allow yourself to be guided by the four elements: air, fire, water, and earth. If we're working with those associations, we have much potential symbolism available to us to wade through, in which to ground ourselves and take root.

What about our mind do we appreciate? How about our drive and motivation? What about our emotions? What about our physical body and our ability to provide for ourselves? How can you represent these different parts of yourself visually, or with objects?

Maybe a photo of yourself as a child, maybe a photo of yourself now. Maybe a print of a painting you've done. Maybe a copy of your diploma or last semester's grades, even if they weren't that great. Maybe a medal or award you've earned (even if it was last place, or one similar to what I was given as a kid – 'Most Unhappy Camper,' a true testament to how much of a city person I have always been). Maybe a photo of the last meal you made for yourself, maybe a gym selfie or a picture of you at a routine hospital visit for a chronic health condition. Maybe it's a bunch of pink things. Maybe green. Maybe it's the necklace you wear every day. Your favourite makeup brush. Maybe it's a collection of seashells you found on your last trip. A copy of a validating diagnosis. It can be big or small.

What makes you feel strong? seen? cared for? acknowledged – on a deep level, not a superficial level?

How can you honour yourself?

Flowers are common on my altar, gifts to my saints, to my animal spirit guides, the genus loci spirits of the land, my holy dead, and any other spirits who are with me. When I make altars for me, I offer flowers in gratitude for myself, in gratitude for the spirit relationships that have shielded me and helped me survive. What helps you to feel the most seen and heard? Do that for yourself, and honour it. Cook your favourite meal (or order your favourite delivery pizza), put some on a plate on the altar as an offering to your spirits, to yourself. Nourish yourself. Offerings can be simple – a glass of tap water is free but overflowing with symbolism. You don't need to buy anything new or spend money to make this happen, though you certainly can if it's within your budget!

Add something new to the altar every day, little by little, or make a big event of it on the night of the full moon.

Enjoy the process: loving and celebrating yourself are not chores! A lot of ritual may be about acquiring this or that thing or shift, but allow this process to be simple, quiet, still, small, peaceful, without expectations. Accept all of your feelings about the process, accept your own energy and where you're at. Notice what's easy. Notice what's not.

Looking at your relationship to yourself is so crucial: the cornerstone of all magical practice is, of course, you.

Celebrate all that you are, all that you bring to the table. Sit with your self long enough, and I promise you'll see a shift in your relationship not only to your self, but to your witchcraft.

RELEASING TRAUMA WITH LITTLE RITUALS

Content note: rape, sexual assault, sexual violence, gender-based violence

Years ago on Valentine's Day, I was very single and recently raped.

I spent the day flying back from Montreal after performing at an occult poetry event put on by a university, and I spent the evening creating an altar devoted to healing my recent rape. I asked my friends and community at large to donate pink candles and other items for me to put on my altar as a big collaborative magic-making ritual full of everyone's energies – pink flowers, anti-rape stickers, and more than 30 pink candles.

Valentine's Day is supposed to be about love, and almost two weeks to the day after that rape I wanted to channel love for myself – and also energy and concern from friends and caring strangers – into my wounds. I want to offer some thoughts on how you can work with a similar swirl of energies in your own practice, particularly during a new moon.

Whatever your relationship to love, I invite you – if it resonates – to work with the next new moon to reflect on and release any pain and trauma that are the result of sexual and gender-based violence. (If you don't have any – awesome, that's great! If you feel called, I feel this approach to ritual could be applied successfully to any kind of unhappiness or trauma.)

Like it or not, our experiences with trauma – particularly involving intimate partner violence and sexual violence – often influence our connection to and access to love, care, and intimacy. In order to better our relationships with ourselves and our loved ones, it is crucial to examine the traumas that persist in our bodies. #MeToo has hit the world, the media and the internet by storm, and though there are so many amazing effects of this movement, it has largely come at the expense of the extensive and painful labouring of women, feminine, non-binary, and gender non-conforming people: people who experience the heavy weight of gender-based violence and non-stop coercive sexualisation in a patriarchal society. Many of us have – again and again – shared our traumas, often at great cost to ourselves; we repeat and relive in the hopes that one more witnessing will give us absolution or will finally give others cause to believe us. The tides are, I hope, shifting. What happens next is still to be seen.

Where I live, trauma therapy is difficult to come by, and it's often not great. Without access to trauma-focused mental health resources, and while living in a country where sexual assault is rampant and yet conviction of perpetrators is abysmally low, I did not and do not find going through the court system or contacting police to be positive and affirming choices for me. I don't want to have my character assassinated, my therapist's notes subpoenaed, my style of dress and choice of lipstick or sexual habits examined. I fear that I would be physically unsafe were I to press charges; my rapist lived across the street from one of the places that I worked at the time.

So what do I do?
Where did I turn?
Witchcraft.
Magic.

Today, I'd like to leave you with a little exercise: an invitation, an opportunity, a moment of stillness and rest.

You can't get rid of all of your trauma with just one spell.

It's a process; one that is long and drawn out, and one best used in conjunction with other healing modalities, such as (but not limited to) finding solace in community and friendship, talk therapy, trauma-informed therapy, EMDR, yoga, theatre, movement, exercise, meditation, and eating and sleeping in ways that support and solidify our health.

Like anything else, witchcraft is rarely a quick fix pill, especially if you are at the beginning of your journey in learning to speak its languages.

However, we have to begin, and with each breath we can release.

Summon up some trauma in your body – remember it.

That may seem like a strange instruction, but stay with me here for a moment. Work with your own awareness of what you can tolerate and what you can't, what you're ready to face and what you're not. Start small. How were you triggered by the #metoo conversations? Were you? For me, that brought up a lot of feelings about peoples' lack of belief(s) in my reported rape(s), and people telling me what I should have done (called the police, pressed charges, not consumed alcohol, not have gone on a date, not have used Tinder, etc), and that what I did/n't do invalidated my rape as rape. Invalidated my pain. They said I was a bad victim, my story not sad enough, somehow my fault. Even the rape crisis line I called told me this after I broke down crying, recounting my story.

I invite you to locate something you have the capacity to face and sit with.

Summon it.

It can be any number of things; maybe it is the disappointment in a friend who didn't show up for you after you were assaulted; maybe it is how stressed out you feel when reading endless celebrity stories about #metoo on your news feed. Maybe it's your own sense of shame around being on Tinder in the first place, about being OK with sex on a first date, or having an interest in rough sex. Find a feeling – big, small, medium sized – that has been occupying more brain space lately than you'd like it to.

I know it may be tempting to want to try to throw the whole thing away at once, but trust me: small, manageable goals work best here.

Found that thing?

Okay good. Now let it go.

How?

Embed whatever that feeling is, that memory, that cluster of thoughts, and put it somewhere.

You can locate it in your exhale, and imagine this thing's hold on your heart, body, mind, and soul leaving you bit by bit with each letting go of breath, and with each inhale you can imagine your body filling with nourishment (or whatever word or symbol of goodness feels nice to you). You can also choose to embody this feeling, memory, or thought cluster in an object. You can write your heart out on a piece of paper, rip it into pieces, set it on fire, and flush it down the toilet.

What symbolizes getting rid of something for you? For some it may involve burning, for some it may involve flushing, or throwing it in the garbage or down a sewer drain at a nearby intersection. You could also hold a candle and charge it with the energy of what you want to release, imagining the thing's hold over you disappearing with the candle wax as it burns.

Water more your style? Take a cleansing shower with herbs of your choice (I love cedar for very intense banishing work), and imagine each stream of water washing away the thing as it massages your flesh and drips down your hair. Imagine your shower water taking the power of this thing with it as it swirls down the drain.

There are so many different ways to work with symbolisms of renewal and banishing around the new moon, the dark moon, the shadow moon. Release. For best effect, I find magical work around trauma responds well to repetition. Try doing whatever action you have chosen every day for one week. Or maybe it's every Saturday morning, every Friday night. Listen to how it feels, and let your heart lead.

Chipping away at trauma – even with magic – isn't a one-shot quick fix. It requires continued commitment. It may be big; it may be a lot.

But I believe magic can help us start somewhere, can help us commit to silence, reflection, screaming, intention, action.

A reminder that we manifest, we make ourselves, shape our worlds.

We cannot change what we have been given by life and birth, but when we work with magic, we acknowledge we have the tools to change our inherited circumstances, to do and be differently in the small steps necessary to change how we feel long-term.

Long-term change is the result of many small shifts. This may sound corny as fuck, but even setting aside the time to breathe through, reflect, and release these experiences and reaffirm our resilience can have a cumulatively powerful effect on our bodies: we remind ourselves that our lives are precious, we are important, we are worth it, and we are enough.

We are still here, and we survived.

And that is worth celebrating.

COMMUNITY WITCHCRAFT

Group work ain't for everyone. But if it's something that calls to you, heed the call!

When you're ready, and with folks you trust, you can try out various ritual techniques in your own community spaces. Maybe at a dinner party with three close friends, or before you begin teaching preschoolers in the morning, before they all arrive.

Try this stuff out in public. Silently. Loudly. Notice it. Fuck up. Try again. Try again. If it helps, make notes. Ask folks how they felt, consider how you felt.

In a ritual setting, the following exercises can be done either solo, or with a group. I suggest the facilitator or host does a few of these exercises in preparation to host the ritual, and then some can be done with all participants present, so that everyone contributes to owning and transforming the space they inhabit. These techniques are great ways to set the stage for manifesting thoughtful and transformative community space. Feel free to adapt these examples as you see fit. Or, find inspiration from the rituals I have created to come up with some ideas of your own.

Before any ritual can be carried out successfully, the space first needs to be shifted and entered into with intention, so that the energy raised is in alignment with that intention and does not become scattered. We don't 'create' energy—we just notice what's already present where we are, and work with it, which is why the language I use in this book centers around the idea of 'shift.'

If you've taken on the role of sole facilitator in an open community group (that is, a group where you don't already know everyone present), you may want to engage in these actions alone, prior to the arrival of your group. Or, depending on the comfort level of the participants, you may want to engage in some of these activities as a group, and reclaim the space together. This can be a great way to build bonds within a group, but also has the potential to alienate participants who are less explicitly spiritual. However, one way to work with that potential area of discomfort is to encourage participants to interpret things in whatever way they like. If they wish to perceive these activities as very literal spiritual cleansings, that's great; if they prefer to see it as metaphorical (functioning in the way a placebo does), that's fine too. If in doubt, ask—and try to work together as a group to figure out something that is comfortable for everyone.

Something else to consider when planning a communal ritual is the needs of your participants. Does anyone have any (dis)abilities that require attention? Does the venue need to be wheelchair accessible? Are there participants who would prefer to sit on chairs rather than the floor? Is the ritual going to be open-invite or closed to a select group of participants? Will the ritual be a space for only women? Only men? Only trans people? Only people of color? Only survivors of assault? Only residents of a certain neighborhood or community? Only people with disabilities? What's the purpose of including or excluding? How does this contribute to group purpose and intention?

We all need our space to heal and work together in a community setting, and thinking about who the space is for might help you and your group set it up in a more intentional way. However, it's important to be aware that exclusive group spaces can be both nurturing and destructive. Both open and closed rituals have their advantages and drawbacks and fulfill different roles in healing and community building.

Something else to think about when creating a ritual is who will be involved in the drafting of it. As the facilitator, will you come up with something and hope everyone likes it? Sometimes it isn't possible to get everyone's opinion, such as when rituals are open-invite and created last minute, as an inspired response to something urgent in the community. If you're working with a smaller group of more experienced practitioners with an egalitarian bent, it might be pertinent to check in with everyone participating. You can brainstorm together, and work on creating a ritual structure together based on active feedback from the group and their preferences and desires. If you have a working group that meets often, try loosening your reins on the operation and allowing less experienced group members to create a ritual outline, and invite them to facilitate.

SAMPLE GROUP RITUALS

These rituals may be used as they are presented here, but I suggest making adaptations to perfectly suit the needs of you and the group you will be working with, whether it's a close-knit group of friends you know well, or an offering you're making to the larger community, with people you may not know quite as well. The ritual structure won't break or explode if you change something, so feel free to explore, and try new things. If something doesn't work for you or your group, try something different next time. Play and experiment. Flow with your energy, feel the vibes, and see where it takes you.

Remember that all involved are learners, and all involved are teachers. Having a group facilitator may be important to keep everything running smoothly and assure that the energy is kept in check, but try to switch up roles frequently and invite everyone to participate. The energy of a non-hierarchical group can be a beautiful and transformative thing, but is definitely not right for everybody. Some groups may benefit from having a leader, and others may not. It depends on the aims and motivations of each group. Hoping for egalitarianism can be nice, but there is such a thing as too many cooks in the kitchen. There's nothing wrong with preferring one style over another for yourself, at different points in your life and processes of growth as a practitioner.

A RITUAL FOR GROUP HEALING

This is a tricky topic. 'Healing' has become contentious, cliché, and overwrought in many contemporary witchy spaces; it sometimes seems as though everyone and their dog is the next hot self-proclaimed healer of all ills and pains. It can be challenging to create space for processing and healing, and it is a big responsibility as well. Every participant in a ritual like this may have something different to heal from. How can we anticipate that and make space for it, as facilitators and space-holders?

Depending on the comfort level of participants with one another, some folks may feel comfortable disclosing, while others may not. It is important to ensure the space remains as 'safe' and comfortable throughout the ritual as can be, though it is always impossible to ever guarantee truly safe space for everyone at once no matter what. What heals one may trigger another.

On that note, I've started to move away from a solely 'safe spaces' framework, and into one where spaces are brave, vulnerable, courageous – and where participants feel safe enough to be real, raw, truthful, and to challenge themselves and sometimes even each other.

The focus of a rite like this should not be that of a talk-therapy session (that's its own specific thing – I love therapy, but prefer to leave that to the experts in that field to facilitate group therapy sessions).

Instead, a ritual can involve working together in a ritualized setting to engage with the beautiful technology of communal magic to work towards healing and support, for each individual and for the group, without the need or pressure to disclose. It may be useful to have a designated 'support person' for practitioners to speak with privately for emotional support in case anything big and hard does come up in the moment. Ensure that person knows how to hold space for others, and is able to simply witness without trying to fix or authoritatively give advice, particularly without consent – not everyone is looking to be told what to do, some folks just want to share and be heard without judgement.

Materials:
- Water
- Salt
- Bowl
- Small bowl
- Ball of yarn (pink)**
- Rose petals*
- Scissors
- Music
- Blankets or pillows to sit on (optional)

Why rose petals?
In my own association of rose petals with love, I draw upon a deep history of writing and mythology on love in the Western world, where roses are often associated with love – romantic love, in particular. I like to work with this symbolism and extend its meaning into self-love and self-care. Roses have a sweet, soft scent and are quite fragrant! The sweetness of their scent makes me think of doing kind things to myself (treating myself with sweetness) and how nourishing that can be. Roses are also a more expensive flower, and this decadence can be drawn upon to increase our sense of self-worth. I'd be remiss if I didn't mention the rose's thorns. For me, a big part of healing from trauma and learning to love myself has been about discernment, about learning to have boundaries, and learning to repair my own alarm system; learning to be powerful and sweet like the rose flower itself, and also learning to grow my own thorns to protect myself and discern between who is safe and who is dangerous – and to be able to prick anyone dangerous should they come too close! On a personal note, rose is one of my most best plant allies!

**Why a pink ball of yarn?*
In my own process, love has been a crucial element of healing from pain, trauma, heartbreak, and violence. In my cultural context, red is often associated with love. Pink is a softer colour (red plus white), less romantic and overtly sexual; red can be evoked to represent and stir up the hot fire of passion. To me, pink represents self-love and self-care. Not into pink, or perhaps you'd prefer to go the multi-coloured route? No problem. The point is that whatever colour(s) you choose should represent and evoke for you and those involved, the idea of self-love and self-care, as well as community care, community healing, and togetherness. (If you want to evoke another vibe with your yarn colour choice – like, say, peace or resilience – I completely support your creativity! Go for it! This ritual suggestion is about and for you, not me!) If you have worries that pink may be too gendered for folks, I recommend having an open discussion with the group before you begin, in which a yarn choice is collectively chosen. If this is the route you'd prefer to go, come prepared with 3-5 colour choices for folks to choose from. Or, maybe you'd like to use multi-coloured rainbow yarn, to represent all the different facets of healing. Go wild! Move from intentionality, thoughtfulness, and intuition.

This ritual was specifically created for a small group of people who may or may not know each other, but who may feel they require healing in their lives. This ritual contains some explanations and is written with the expectation that most participants may be new to magic and ritual. The phrasing and structure used are for the context of a full moon, but you can easily adapt it to any other moon phase (or some other way of marking time) if you wish.

Before participants arrive, begin to energetically transform the space by visualizing a healing light pink ball of energy around the room. Sprinkle salt water around the parameters of the room in order to cleanse it, while saying something like (either aloud or silently), "By water and earth, healing is birthed." Yeah, that sounds pretty corny, I know—but remember, the exact words matter less than your intention. A short semi-rhyming phrase may help you be more engaged, as it will serve as a reminder of what you're doing and why. It's easier to remember. Feel free to make this up on the spot and be as casual or old-timey in your language as you wish. Working with water and salt also connects the rite to the two big receptive elements in Western magic: earth and water. They can work with you to help your efforts in linking the space to the active reception of cleansing and healing.

Once all participants have arrived, ask everyone to grab a few handfuls of rose petals from a bowl and stand in a circle. Circles are non-hierarchical and emphasize the equality and kinship of all participants. One by one, ask each person to introduce themselves, say why they are present, and what they hope to gain from the ritual. After each participant is finished speaking, they will step a few feet outside the circle and scatter the rose petals on the perimeter of the circle. Once finished, they should return to their spot, and allow each participant in turn to continue the same process, though it is recommended that each person begins speaking as soon as the previous person has finished. Otherwise there might be a lot of self-conscious staring at folks sprinkling rose petals, and it's supposed to be a semi-private meditative exercise for individuals when they are doing it. The facilitator can explain that as each of us do this, we are energetically and physically merging our intentions to the space, individually and as a group, so that the conversations we have and magic we do may better serve us and suit our goals and needs.

All participants sit. The facilitator brings out a pink ball of yarn. For this part of the ritual, each participant will say one thing that they feel has been an impediment to their healing. When someone wishes to speak next, the ball of yarn is thrown to them (make sure that they are ready to catch it!), and then they throw it to the next speaker. This should look a bit like a web. If someone drops it or needs help with this, no problem – I'm not the most coordinated person myself! Once everyone has finished listing perceived impediments to their healing process, the facilitator introduces the next aspect of this exercise.

Then, a pair of scissors will be passed around, and participants are invited to cut the yarn between each connection (the thread of yarn between two participants would equal one connection) when they offer ideas and suggestions to facilitate healing for themselves, and/or the group as a whole—basically, ways to overcome some of the impediments or challenges participants brought up in the first part of the exercise. This section of the ritual is based on practical solutions—i.e., remain accountable to another buddy in the ritual, or make time for journaling every Sunday night before bed. Encourage the group to keep making suggestions until all links in the web are broken.

Then, invite participants to evenly divide up the lengths of yarn. Ensure that each participant has three or more lengths, even if it means cutting up some more of the yarn used to make the web. Do not grab more yarn that was unused. Turn on some music, and lead the group in braiding the yarn together. Let the conversation wander, but try to ensure it focuses roughly on the topic of healing.

Once everyone is finished braiding, it is time to do a big raising of energy. Turn on some music that everyone agrees to, dim the lights (if you like), and have a healing dance party! The music you play doesn't specifically have to be about healing, but the focus of this aspect of the ritual should be about feeling happy and comfortable in our own skin—which is necessary for healing of many types. Be sure that participants hold onto their yarn braids while dancing. When everyone's all danced out, the yarn has been charged with healing vibes. Magic!

Through dancing and movement, the yarn talismans have been charged and become potent. Encourage participants to hang the yarn braid on their wall, somewhere that they can see it every day as a reminder of their commitment to their healing journey. You can suggest that people put it on a bag as a keychain, or to wear it as a bracelet. Whenever I've tried this, the braid lasted only a few days before falling off by itself as I was just living life, and I quickly forgot about it—but this has its own power, too. Allowing the yarn to separate from your being when it is ready can be a powerful symbol of healing, release, and moving on.

Close the circle with any of the grounding techniques suggested in this book.

A Ritual for Reclaiming Public Space

This ritual was written for the purpose of reclaiming a public park after repeated sexual assaults in or near that space; inspired by events in my old neighbourhood a few years ago.

It is written in such a way that it is suitable to be performed during any moon phase, though I would recommend doing it on a Tuesday, at roughly the time of day when the assaults had taken place. Each day of the week has different energetic associations, and Tuesday has long been thought to be ruled by Mars and what I'd call 'go-get-em and fuck shit up' battle warrior energies. If you need to do magic which involves fighting back, resisting, or rebelling, Tuesday is your day, according to Western style magical correspondences, but this ritual can really be done at any time – even on a Saturday, for a darker energy, as Saturday has associations with the deity Saturn.

For this ritual you should have, at the very least, a small core group of very experienced energy workers and magical practitioners to carry out the skeleton of the ritual and to keep group energy focused and on task; this can help to pull folks back into the fold who may feel activated or upset as different feelings bubble up for them.

As long as you have that small core group, you can open this ritual up to the public as an open-invite event. I recommend being careful about who you tell and where you advertise, if you do—nothing ruins a ritual more than folks who just want to fuck with what you're doing and make fun of your healing and reclamation process. Otherwise, though, the more the merrier! You may want to reach out to survivors, victims of assaults, friends, family, and supportive people who live in the neighborhood. Though the bones of this ritual are tied together by a small group of experienced practitioners, the focus should be on fostering community engagement and reclaiming ownership of shared community space. Use your judgement and discretion.

Since the work being done in this ritual is difficult, it may be wise to plan for any potential outbursts of emotion. In addition to keeping the energy on track during the ritual itself, members in the small group should have a step-by-step process planned should any participants be triggered, feel unsafe, or visibly upset during the ritual.

How will this situation be mitigated? What resources and actions will you plan to use to assist this person? If no assistance is wanted, they may wish to leave, or simply have some alone time. Defer to what they say will help them feel supported, and always be sure to ask if they would like your help and what their immediate needs are.

You may wish to have a designated support person, and designated space nearby to bring individuals to calm down, regroup, or receive support, just in case. It's likely that this won't be necessary, but it's always preferable to be prepared, especially when intense energy work of this nature is being done.

Some participants may have wounds that are still very fresh. Respect their process, and the form and pace it takes.

Materials:
- Bowls
- Mason jars
- Mini mirrors
- Balls of coloured yarn
- Rain water or snow (ideal), or tap water (will do in a pinch)

Depending on the time of year and where you live, the small core group should collect rainwater or snow in preparation for the ritual. Get as much of this as you can! And don't pick it up from the street; leave out cups or bowls to collect it as it falls from the sky. Leaving out one mason jar may seem poetic, but trust me, it won't do the job—leave out as many as you can. I'd recommend bowls with a wide brim so you can increase your collection area and get more snow or rain. If you are collecting snow, let it melt. The more you can collect the better, especially if the space you're looking to reclaim is large. You may need to do multiple collections to get enough.

If you're not in a season or place where it's likely to rain or snow when you're hoping to do this ritual, no worries—in a pinch, tap water will do, maybe even with some ice in it!

Sometimes, I'll leave out jars to collect rain or snow, even when I'm not too sure how or when I'll use it in ritual. You can always keep it for later so you're prepared!

Personally, I like to periodically collect rain water as well as snow for later work with in ritual, so that I'm prepared for when occasions to use these special forms of water present themselves. I think there is something really beautiful and symbolic about magically working with a form of water that has not yet made contact with the earth, if you catch it before it hits the ground! Rain, especially, comes directly from clouds, from the sky, and rainfall is something I have always held as energetically aligned with cleansing and washing away of nasty energies. Once that rain water hits the ground, it changes. Snow is another opportunity to work with falling water (in solid form), and also adds on the potential to work with the concept of 'thaw' in our magical work.

For instance, sexual assault occurring in a park quite often can make that place feel frozen in time, or the energy of that space somehow stuck. To work with the concept of energetically unfreezing something, of warming it up and making it comfortable and community oriented again, I like the energetic and symbolic associations that open up here when we work with snow.

Again, that's just an ideal for the symbolism I'm trying to work with in this ritual; feel free to improvise—you can always choose to just use ice from your freezer and thaw it yourself, if the thawing out concept resonates with you and the situation you're working with.

As a small group, you can charge the water and as many colorful balls of yarn as you can reasonably afford for the purpose of re-energizing and reclaiming the park as a safe and nurturing space.

Purchase little mirrors and charge them, as well—but with a different purpose. You want to infuse the mirrors with reflective energy. Visualize the little mirrors as reflective shields that don't absorb negative energy, but instead dissipate it and can return to sender.

Leave enough time before the formal ritual to perform one additional task as a small group. Walk around the perimeter of the park, clockwise, while sprinkling the collected water as you go. Be sure to conserve enough to last you the entire journey around the park—this may vary widely based on the size of the location in question.

While you do this, imagine and visualize the water being soaked into the ground, strengthening the space, revitalizing it, cleansing it of negative, harmful, and violent energetic residues. The purpose of doing this before additional participants arrive is to lay a strong energetic foundation for the ritual.

Since it is open invite, many folks may show up who are unfamiliar with energy shielding and protecting themselves prior to and while encountering violent energy. These people may begin to feel sick, get headaches, or become dizzy or claustrophobic, and not know why. Additionally, laying this foundation in a small group rather than in a large crowd will ensure that participants feel like participants in the main ritual, rather than just bystanders of a performance you're doing.

Once all participants have arrived, you may wish to explain why you have chosen to engage the community in a ritual for the reclamation of public space. Much of this may not need to be said, given the circumstances and who is present, but it may be pertinent to say a few words of solidarity, encouragement, and support, as well as to outline the ritual's itinerary and to point out any designated support people. Many people with trauma may not be fond of surprises and generally like to know what they're getting themselves into.

As a group, circle the perimeter of the park clockwise, wrapping yarn around any poles, streetlights, benches, fences, bike racks, and other inorganic structures. Explain the allure of yarn for this project; it's soft, comforting, colorful, and friendly, and so is a natural representative of safe space. Yarn bombing the park is a literal and magical act of reclaiming it. After one round has been done, encourage participants to wander into the park and affix yarn to additional built structures (as the growth of trees and plants may be negatively impacted by yarn wrapping). Give out some of the mirrors to participants to affix to larger poles on the outskirts of the park, and encourage them to trap the mirrors beneath layers and layers of yarn, so they stay firmly in place. Once a ball of yarn is finished, the end of the string should be tied to yarn already on the structure, so the yarn doesn't unravel. As you pass out the mirrors, be sure to explain their purpose, as well, so participants know why they are doing what they're doing. There's nothing worse than thoughtless actions in any type of ritual!

After the yarn and mirrors are all affixed to structures, gather everyone on the most convenient patch of grass or cluster of benches, or even playground equipment, and encourage everyone to share a positive, happy story or memory of an experience they had in the park. Funny or lighthearted stories are the best, and can help keep the energy high. If the group is especially large, you may wish to suggest participants break off into small groups, or to pair up with someone they have never met before.

To complete the ritual, ask for parade leaders for one last hurrah around the park's perimeters. You may ask them to lead a chant or to sing a song—anything works! The words of the song matter less than the positive energy participants feel from singing and marching in solidarity with new friends and old friends alike.

With the final march around the park, the ritual is complete. You may wish to encourage folks to grab drinks or food with you afterwards—or both! Sharing in nourishment together can help lighten the mood, solidify social bonds, create new connections (and deepen old ones), and eating is super grounding for the physical body. I love eating after ritual – it brings me back down to earth.

CREATING YOUR OWN RITUALS

It's powerful to create your own rituals.

A ritual isn't more legitimate or authentic just because you read it in a book – even this one!

The symbols, spirits, and ways of doing and being that resonate strongly with me may not resonate very much with you, if they do at all – and, thus, carbon copying my sample rituals may feel good to you, and it may not!

For some of you, trying some of what I've described may help you get in touch with your own magic; for others of you, it might just be nice to see these as launching points for your own inspiration and ritual creation.

It might feel scary to create your own rituals, but chances are, you're already doing this, at least to some extent, all the time! We ritualize daily life – when we cook, clean our bodies and homes, get ready to go out, exercise, work, love, and play. We can bring these ritual skills with us as we begin to construct our own spiritual and magical rituals, and experiment with and explore what magical ritual might look like in our own personal context.

When you're thinking of creating your own rituals, it may be useful to use some of the sections in this chapter as guidelines or guideposts. Here are some questions that might be helpful to contemplate:

What is your current relationship to daily, mundane, everyday ritual?

What types of rituals do you enjoy – cooking, cleaning, bathing, applying skincare or makeup, selecting what to wear?

Do you have any fun daily rituals that ground you, like getting a coffee every morning or going for a walk? How can you infuse more explicit magic, intention, and spiritual awareness into these rituals you already do?

Otherwise, you might feel called to think about magical timing, and your own relationship to daily cycles – the sun, the moon, the stars; monthly cycles, annual cycles, seasonal cycles – how would you map out your own relationship(s) to time?

When does it feel good to practice, when does it not?

What moments do you feel inspired to honour, for yourself, for your community?

Do you feel more called to solitary ritual? Group ritual? Or, perhaps both?

Are you more aligned with ritual that is deeply structured and organized, or with magic that is more wild, spontaneous, uninhibited? What does that look like for you, in your context? Or, if it feels better, how might you bring these approaches together, meld them into something so very uniquely you?

It can be a little scary the first time we create our own ritual – choose our own correspondences for colour, time, and spirit collaborators; our own structure and words and movements.

But this is also the beginning of strengthening connection to our own spiritual power in our magical practice.

Above all, trust yourself, trust your intuition, and see where it leads you!

Claim your magic.

Change your life.

xoxo Sabrina

thank you

Thank you so much for taking the time to read this book. I appreciate you! A huge thank you to my audience, fans, and supporters over the years, I would not have gotten this far without all of you. Some of you have been following my journey and my work since 2011, and it is you, your belief and confidence in me and what I have to say that has given me strength and confidence as each year has gone by.

To my first cohorts of Tarot Without Bullshit and Magic Without Bullshit students back in 2019 and 2020: thank you for helping me believe and know in my bones that I can do this.

Massive gratitude to Maria Vicente, without whom this book would not be what it is. Our countless conversations over the years have been priceless. Big thank you to everyone in writing club - especially Lainey Cameron and Charlotte Dune - I love you all. To all of my friends who have put up with me complaining about this process: thank you. A huge thank you as well to my amazing assistant Cait Linden, for taking on responsibilities that gave me more time to finish this project.

Thank you, as well, to all my haters - to every publishing house who rejected this book, as well as to the publishers that did want it but with whom it didn't work out. Adversity just gives me more belief in my work, and more confidence that my voice needs to be out in the world. This work wouldn't be what it is without you, either.

And, of course, last but not least - thank you to my home, to my three beautiful cats, and my entire spirit team, my ancestors, saints, and all of my spirit guides, in all forms - animal, plant, mineral, place, and more. Thank you to the waves, the skyscrapers, the seagulls, the train, the pigeons, the garbage trucks, the sidewalk dandelions. You all held me and make my life and this book possible. Thank you to my body, my mind, my soul. Thank you, thank you, thank you.

about Sabrina

Sabrina Scott is a globally recognized professional witch and spiritual teacher with more than 20 years of experience, 200+ students, and clientele worldwide. She has been profiled by Vice, Broadly, Refinery29, Yahoo, Witches Magazine, Sabat Magazine, Clin d'oeil Magazine, Ghosts Magazine, and more. She is an artist, writer, and speaker.

Sabrina is known for her sassy, iconoclastic, no bullshit style of spiritual teaching on topics as diverse as witchcraft, magic, tarot, divination, energy work, animism, mediumship, environmental spirituality, manifestation, affirmations, and the power of feminine energy. She offers bespoke mentorship services in creativity, spirituality, magic, tarot, business, and personal transformation.

Her purpose is to inspire others to claim their magic and radically transform their lives, and she leads by example. Sabrina has overcome some of the darkest experiences life has to offer, and by sharing her experience and process, she aims to inspire and teach others to do the same - to find their own magic, and change their life.

She is the creator of graphic novel *Witchbody*, which was nominated for the biggest comics award series in Canada. *Witchbody* has received praise from environmental philosopher Timothy Morton, comics journalist Joe Sacco, tarot gurus Rachel Pollack and Michelle Tea, and acclaimed witch Judika Illes.

Curse and Cure is Sabrina's second book.

find me online

Sabrina's Website:

https://sabrinamscott.com

Social Media:

Instagram: instagram.com/sabrinamscott
Youtube: youtube.com/sabrinascott
Tiktok: tiktok.com/thesabrinamscott
Twitter: twitter.com/sabrinamscott

My courses

Tarot: sabrinamscott.com/tarot-courses

Tarot Without Bullshit: Ten modules. Twenty hours of video content. Ten massive worksheets. This course will take you from confused (or insecure) to expert tarot reader. Many students have successfully launched tarot businesses after taking this course. My most jam-packed and advanced tarot offering. Don't memorize: actually learn how to make tarot relevant to you and your life, so you can read with confidence for life.

Tarot at the End of the World: This three hour masterclass is a great primer on some of the toughest cards in the deck - those that come up a lot during and as we recover from a global pandemic. If you're afraid of the tarot and 'bad' cards, this is a great choice for you. Learn to be fearless with tarot.

Tarot Boss: This three hour masterclass is great for those looking to take their tarot practice pro. Learn the foundations of a solid and lucrative professional tarot practice, as well as the pillars of social media, branding, cultivating brave spaces for your clients, and more.

Witchcraft and Magic: sabrinamscott.com/magic-courses

Magic Without Bullshit: Ten modules. Twenty four hours of video content. Ten massive worksheets. Take your magical practicee from tepid and nonspecific to personal, powerful, potent, and alive. Jam-packed modules on cosmology and belief are the foundation of this powerful nondenominational course on witchcraft. Magical mechanics are discussed in depth, as well as an intensive module on candle magic. My most extensive course.

Visualizing Energy Work: This two hour workshop and thirty minute question and answer session teaches you how to make energy work feel and look more real to you through a series of guided energy work practices followed by colouring and drawing exercises. Energy work is the foundation of all witchcraft, magic, and spiritual practice, but it is often too abstract to learners for it to feel real and useful. Overcome that block in this workshop.

Self Transformation: sabrinamscott.com/self-transformation

Claim Your Magic Affirmation Series: If affirmations, manifestation, and positve psychology feel alien to you, this series of six affirmations - as well as a handful of anchoring audio instruction to teach you how to best make use of the affirmations - is a great place to begin. It may seem simple, but affirmations can completely shift your consciousness and begin to plant the seeds of seismic change. A great place to get your spiritual toes wet.

Witchcraft, Feminine Energy, and Plastic Surgery: In this two hour masterclass, I teach about my experiences with feminine energy, feminine embodiment, plastic surgery, and witchcraft - including an in-depth share of all of the spiritual techniques and witchy practices I used to prepare for my surgery, both months before and day of. A very vulnerable and powerful session that demonstrates how to put my spiritual teachings into practice to support something as intense as gender affirming elective surgery.

witchbody

"Sabrina Scott's *Witchbody* is a welcome and much needed reminder of the sheer physicality inherent in witchcraft and of the power and pleasure which that provides. Magic is in your body and in all bodies; human and non-human alike. *Witchbody* will ground your witchcraft practices and recalibrate your magical vision. It has benefit for all readers but especially for the modern witch."
— Judika Illes, author of *Encyclopedia of Witchcraft*, *Encyclopedia of 5000 Spells*, and other books of magic

"Cerebral, passionate, and beautifully drawn, Sabrina Scott's *Witchbody* invites us to consider our connection not just to nature but to what we normally consider outside of nature. A highly distinctive and engaging book."
— Joe Sacco, comics journalist, author of *Palestine*, *Footnotes in Gaza*, and more

The first graphic novel of its kind, *Witchbody* is a meandering synthesis of autoethnography, magic theory, and philosophical speculation. It is full of wonder at what it can mean to learn and teach and change and grow in this world which belongs to all of us: you, me, plants, trees, coffee cups and garbage bins. What can it mean to be a witch today, in the city?

I wanted to make something that was an exhale containing my soul, and so I decided to make a comic book about magic. Magic is my lifeblood, it is my lens, it is how I feel and interact with others. It is all of those things, and more. This book is an illustrated essay about how techniques of magic can re-orient the practitioner to see non-human bodies and relationships in different ways. Part activist, part academic, part rant, part poetry, part magic: all illustrated.

My practices as an illustrator, writer, and witch are all intermingling, entangled. These creative processes are my way of working out similar things using different methods and media, but the creative fire that emerges comes from the same inspiration and intuition. I want to help push forward conversations about magic, life, death, change, transformation, environment, learning, growing.

I want to help us see our own stories, and to encourage the writing of new ones.
I created this book to be a talisman.
Will you accept its invitation?

what to do next

Check out my courses, workshops, and masterclasses: Ok, you've read the book - what next? Wanna learn more? On the previous pages, you'll see information about my various offerings. Surf over to my website, sabrinamscott.com, pick a course or masterclass, and enroll. Keep your momentum going!

Follow me on social media: I almost exclusively exist on Instagram @sabrinamscott - this is the best way to keep up to date on current musings, offerings, and courses, as well as free content and workshops.

Sign up for my newsletter: When you join my newsletter, you'll get tons of awesome witchy content delivered straight to your inbox - as well as my absolutely free *13 Witchy Books* list. You'll get a pop-up invite to do this when you go to my website, sabrinamscott.com, but if you'd like an exact link, here it is: https://mailchi.mp/7f19844d8faa/13witchybooks

Check out my first book, *Witchbody*: If you haven't read *Witchbody*, you should! Less how-to, more philosophical and poetic, this graphic novel shows how I see magic, how I do magic, and what it means to me to be a witch in the city. *Witchbody* is available in bookstores and all over the internet.

Write an Amazon review for *Curse and Cure*: Reviews are huge for self published writers! If you loved this book, please let the world know by leaving a review. It means the world and helps get my work out there!

Printed in Great Britain
by Amazon